∞ Unless Your Faith Is Strong ∞

Our Awesome Ability to Believe and to Believe Strongly Enough to Live, to Learn and to Grow

Donald Horak

Symbol on back cover and inside title page: The Christian symbol of the cross and the universal symbol of faith/affirmation represents spirit, or being, as one and infinite, symbolized by a triangle, a circle and a heart. A variation also has the alpha A – beginning, omega.Ω. – end, and ∞ - infinity embedded The design was finalized in 1999. It is in the public domain.

© 2015 by Donald E. Horak
ISBN-10: 1517653142   ISBN-13: 978-1517653149
        1 - Spirituality 2 – Psychology 3 – Sacraments 4 - Ethics
        5 - Religion and Science

Library of Congress Control Number: 2015918783
LCCN Imprint Name: CreateSpace Independent Publishing Platform
                North Charleston, South Carolina

∞In Loving Memory of Elizabeth and George∞

∞

Dedicated to so many others who have nourished and formed me in faith and ministry.

Contents

Chapter One:
•The power of believing •Still-life and motion pictures •The greatest detriment to faith •The Spirit and the faith of Cornelius and Peter The Spirit and the faith of the church •The Spirit and the faith of believers •The dynamic spirit of faith Signs of this dynamic Spirit.
Bringing the Faith to Life: •The purpose of parables and sacraments •The purpose of ritual •The purpose of sacramental rituals.

Chapter Two:
• Searching for our identity • "In the name of the Father and of the Son and of the Holy Spirit. Amen" •Bringing the Rite to Life.

•The mission—called and sent •"Born again" •Rebirth—Nicodemus and the woman at the well •Rebirth and salvation •Sustaining rebirth and life •Defining words and blessing of baptism •Our human baptismal family. **Bringing the Rite to Life**: •The cross—our sign of faith •Remembering our baptism.

Chapter Four:

Conclusion

•The church and science •What is dark energy? •What is dark matter? •The light of faith and the life of the sacraments •Having that mind which was in Christ Jesus.

Appendix

• Understanding my ability to believe • Understanding my baptismal identity • Understanding my confirmation call • Understanding my Eucharistic call • Understanding the healing grace of reconciling my sinfulness • Understanding the healing grace of anointing my mortality • Understanding the grace of shepherding the home • Understanding the grace of shepherding the church • Conclusion

About the Author

> *The supreme achievement of the self*
> *is to find an insight that connects*
> *together the events, dreams, and*
> *relationships that make up our*
> *existence.*

Leonard Biallas writes this in his book *Myths, Gods, Heroes, and Saviors*. I also came across a reflection attributed to an unknown Confederate soldier. It ended with this statement: "I got nothing that I asked for, but everything I hoped for. Almost despite myself, my unspoken prayers were answered. I am, among all [people], most richly blessed." And although I wasn't looking for such an insight, it found me, and it made connections with significant events, dreams, and relationships in my life.

Ordained a priest of the Diocese of Steubenville in 1963, I was thinking primarily about being in parish ministry (The Bells of St. Mary's). Then I thought about the possibility of becoming a military chaplain (marines, of course, my father was one). But I was asked to prepare to teach. OK! So I was thinking in terms of teaching mathematics, my favorite and easiest subject. I was sent to get a master's degree in classical languages, which I taught for four years until the liturgical language became the vernacular (English). So, then I was asked to get certified to teach mathematics along with social studies (hardly a direct route!). Being somewhat athletic, I thought the students needed a more organized athletic program in order to compete with other schools. I mentioned this to the rector and was named athletic director (really not my intention). I found out they didn'thave books on how to be an athletic director. But, thanks to Fred Bartimoccia, our program developed quite well over time.

After eleven years at the high-school level, I was assigned to our diocesan seminary—college and theology—as instructor in Greek. After ten years that decision needed some reviewing on my part. I was also appointed spiritual director, for which I needed more preparation. Having received the degree in classical languages from Catholic University, returning there seemed the logical choice to get this degree. But I found out that an academic program in spirituality was not quite developed yet. So working toward a master's in psychology and counseling became the goal for the next three summers. During that time our diocese welcomed the Ministry to Priests Program developed by Father Vincent Dwyer, a Trappist monk from St. Joseph Monastery in Spencer, Massachusetts. The program needed priests to volunteer to interpret psychological testing and to do counseling. I was invited to an introductory session for possible volunteers. This led to facilitating retreats in Antigonish, Nova Scotia, St. Louis, Missouri, Lismore, Bribane, and Melbourne, Australia.

After four years, the difficult decision was made to close the diocesan seminary and send the students to other seminaries. When asked where I would like to go, campus ministry at Ohio University wasn't what I was thinking. Twenty-two years as pastor at Christ the King University Parish formed me in ministry in ways I had never dreamed, one of which was to learn enough Spanish to celebrate Mass (thanks, Josepina).

After some serious vision problems, I had various degrees of success in my attempts at retirement. After four years of continuing to help in the parishes in Athens, Ohio, Fr. Ed Bell, a priest from the diocese of Wheeling-Charleston in West Virginia—and a great friend from the days we were on the high-school faculty—and I decided to retire to South Carolina. In order to be of assistance in another diocese, one needs a letter from one's bishop to the bishop of the new diocese stating that one is in good standing. As it turned out, the vicar of priests in Charleston, South Carolina, sent letters to the parishes in the area where we were staying, stating that we were in good standing and would be available to assist if needed.

The first month was quiet. The second month brought invitations fm outlying areas. The third month I received a call from the chief of chaplains, Parris Island, asking if I could help for two weekends as one of the military chaplains had to be away. Not a problem. A couple of weeks later, the chief of chaplains called again and wanted to see me. Long story short, he asked if I would consider being a contract chaplain (civilian, not military) on a year-to-year basis. So, forty-two years after thinking about being a military chaplain, I found myself on Parris Island as a contract chaplain for the marines and recruits. Perhaps I needed those years just to get ready. It was, indeed, a very enriching experience that lasted for seven-plus years.

Mixed in with weekends at Parris Island were retreats for priests, permanent deacons, and various parishes. And then when the priest who was offering Mass in Spanish at the local parish was away, I was asked if I spoke Spanish. I replied *sòlo un poco* (thinking that would put the issue to rest), but it was the beginning of an awesome seven-year experience that I have not yet fully processed or comprehended.

> *I got nothing that I asked for, but everything I hoped for. Almost despite myself, my unspoken prayers were answered. I am, among all [people], most richly blessed.*

About the Book

> *The Christian ideal has not been tried*
> *and found wanting. It has been found*
> *difficult; and left untried.*

G. K. Chesterton expresses this thought in his book, *What's Wrong with the World*. The line comes from part 1, chapter 5, "The Unfinished Temple." So what makes Christianity difficult to the point of being untried? There probably are as many reasons as there are people. From years of listening to people—the majority being eighteen- to thirty-year-olds on one side of the age spectrum and fifty and older on the other side—two underlying causes kept coming up in discussions. The first is that our awareness of our need for faith (i.e., our ability to believe) has disappeared into the background. This, in turn, makes it difficult—if not almost impossible—to come to an experience of the spiritual realities that bring a quality of life to our existence. How can one come to any relationship with another human person if the significant ties that bind them are spiritual and not physical? Most of what nourishes and sustains the human spirit is based on one's ability to believe and trust. Neither one's intellectual nor one's emotional abilities are capable of doing that. And then, when it comes to one's relating to God, how can one relate to a personal God one cannot see, feel, or touch? How can one come to an awareness of being created in the image and likeness of this God?

How much faith does it take? Jesus told the disciples and us that if we had faith the size of a mustard seed, we could handle life. But we have to use that ability, and let it grow. And it will grow, and it will engage us in life in ways beyond our greatest expectations. Faith is ever open to show us meaning in life beyond the superficial and obvious.

We can grow to believe that "God so loved the world, that he sent his only begotten Son" who in turn sent the Spirit into the world. We can grow to believe that all of us are beloved children of God. We can grow to believe that sacraments are life-doors and windows through which we engage in a relationship with God and with one another. We need only to believe enough to bring those sacramental rites to life in ourselves. We need only believe that the realities of faith and sacraments are open-ended realities that make possible an encounter with the divine.

Unless Your Faith Is Strong is a small attempt to refocus on our need to be aware of our awesome ability to believe and the power, life, and grace that flows from believing strongly. The truths of faith are not just something to be known and understood; they are to be lived. The scriptures and sacraments are not just to be listened to and received. They are to be brought to life—realizing that the receiving of a sacrament is not an end but a beginning…In fact it is a beginning that does not end.

> "The Christian ideal has not been tried and found wanting. It has been found difficult; and…" Well, that's up to us now, isn't it?

—Donald Horak

Acknowledgments

My sincere gratitude goes to all whose help, support, and guidance made this book possible. My experience has led me to believe that in some way or another, we are touched and formed by all the people with whom we spend any significant time—as well as people whom we have never met except through their writing or the memories of them that others have shared. I am grateful for having finally realized that as I discover traces of their influence in myself.

I am grateful for the formation I received from the dedication and motivation of teachers at every level of education; from classmates and friends through the years; and family—especially my sisters, Ruth, Rose, Barbara, Carolyn, and Janet, who continue to teach and inspire me.

A great deal of thanks goes to the students I thought I was teaching only to realize how much they were teaching me. The same is true for the people of the various parishes who ministered to me as much or more than I to them: especially the people of Christ the King University Parish and St. Paul's in Athens, Ohio; my ecumenical brothers and sisters in Athens; the people of the Low Country parishes and the Marines and recruits at Parris Island, South Carolina.

I am indebted in so many ways to Ralph Moran, Gary Schumacher, Kathy Schumacher, Roger Menchofer, Jack Docherty, Joyce Hamby, Moira O'Dea, Kathleen Kutsko, James Coady, Father Thomas Magary, Kip Rondy, Mack Ellis, and Anne Herndon who were willing to accept my request to read and give feedback as the manuscript was coming together. It was Gary, Joyce, James, and Moira who took a significant amount of time to question, advise, and correct not only my method of writing but also punctuation and typos. And to Ashley Hahn Calvery for her help with the publishing company. Thanks to all!

All...were by nature foolish who were in ignorance of God, and who from the good things seen did not succeed in knowing the One who is, and from studying the works did not discern the artisan...For if they so far succeeded in knowledge that they could speculate about the world, how did they not more quickly find its Lord? (Wisdom 13:1-2,9)

Prologue

If we are going to invest time, resources and our very selves in life, we want some kind of guarantee that it will be worth our time, resources and our personal self. We want some seal of approval that what we see and come to know is authentic. We want to trust. And we want the faith to believe in our trusting. And we want to believe in our trusting so that we can be in relationship with our world and the other people who dwell here with us. This basic desire to relate is what motivates us across the whole spectrum of our living. And when we cannot trust, our faith in believing and our ability to relate in any authentic way is considerably diminished. Thus we end up not trusting the language we hear or the signs we see and so we might tend to dilute the meaning of our response, if we respond at all. Hardly satisfying and hardly a world worth living in or investing our time and resources.

Our technology has given us numerous and marvelous ways to communicate. And we can do so quickly and to the other side of the world – even far into outer space. But the common denominator to our communication is language: no matter whether the method of communication is verbal, print, body language or signs and symbols.

"Politicians made no discernible sense when they spoke, few doctors used the word 'cancer' with patients who have it, and the word 'immigrant' could no longer be prefaced by 'illegal'. Detach language from meaning, and the world [is] yours."* Donna Leon has Guido Brunetti musing with this mindset as he is trying to make sense of some of the decisions rendered by the court in his home city of Venice where he is a Commissario or Police Inspector.

But if the "language is detached from meaning", then the word, spoken, printed, body language and the signs and symbols will be so much static and those who desire to relate to our world and one another soon lose the will to do so. And the human spirit becomes lonely, frustrated and cynical and thus is unwilling to commit to anything or anyone. Words have meaning and words have power.

Many products we buy and services we engage require us to read a long detailed list of disclaimers. It is as if people are so afraid of taking responsibility for anything. Everything from political promises to labeling products is worded with such vagueness or euphemisms that any essence of meaning gets lost. Detach language from meaning and the world is yours? But then how satisfying would a world without meaning really be? Expedient for the moment? Yes! Much more complex? Yes! Fulfilling in the long run? Hardly!

Jesus knew how critical it was for the human spirit to have trust enough and faith enough to relate to the world and those who live in it. Jesus also knew that the human spirit needed a method of communication deeper than external signs and language and embedded in a power source beyond itself. God has planted in each person a seed of trust, of faith and of relationship, much like a zip file in a computer. But Jesus uses the symbol of a mustard seed instead. As we 'unzip' this file or allow the 'seed' to grow in us, we can connect with the very Word of God which has not lost its meaning.

Father Simon Tugwell O. P. makes this point in "*Prayer: Living with God*":

> *God's word is addressed to us as we really are, not as we like to present ourselves; he speaks to our heart not to our mask. It is not only to that little bit of us which we have, as it were,*

colonized and made subject to our control, that is involved in the Christian enterprise: it is the whole [person]...
God is not taken in by our polite little speeches. [God} knows us through and through, far better than we know ourselves. [God] hears what we are really saying, [God] listens to our heart. And if we would learn to keep company with [God] we must become the kind of people who are prepared to be heard and addressed at that deep level, which requires a great deal of honesty and humility.**

Now how satisfying would that be – to have someone who listens to our heart, who understands us – whose Word has meaning and substance? Jesus tells us that all we need is "faith the size of a mustard seed."

Introduction

"Unless your faith is firm, you shall not be firm" (Isaiah 7:9 NABRE). (See Isaiah 7:1–9 for full context.) This quote is Isaiah's response to King Ahaz when Jerusalem was under attack, and King Ahaz and the people were overcome with fear.

Many people today believe that faith has gone the way of the rotary-dial telephone and other such previously useful items. "You need to get real" is a common response we might hear in our age of science and technology. There's a presumption that faith isn't real. Abstract concepts and problems can be frustrating and a monumental pain. We prefer things that can be seen, measured, touched, and controlled. After all, "Seeing is believing, isn't it?"

There is a tendency to value knowledge as being higher than belief or faith. But what really does come first, faith or knowledge? Does faith lead to knowledge? Does knowledge lead to faith? Can we even come to knowledge without faith? And what sustains knowledge once we have it? I'm not speaking about religious faith at this point. I am referring to our human ability just to believe in general and how we come to know and relate to our world. How much do we *know* and how much do we *have faith* or how much do we *believe*? How much do we have to know before we are on the road to faith? How much faith do we have to have before we are on the road to knowledge?

Belief and faith, though often used interchangeably, are not quite parallel. Belief may or may not imply certitude in the one who assent and faith in its current sense often suggests credulity and overreadiness to accept. For the purpose of this discussion, I would like to suggest a difference that I see between belief and faith.

My grade-school teacher told me, and showed me on a map, that there is a country called China. I chose to believe her because I had faith in her as a teacher. Faith, in this sense, is belief but with the added investment of trust. This trust is something that develops over time in a teacher-student relationship. In this sense it is more than belief, but it is not knowledge. But do we understand and value the fact that it takes a great deal of belief and faith to get us to knowledge? And where exactly is the line which one crosses to move from faith to knowledge? Can one have knowledge of China without experiencing something about China? Then, how much experience is necessary?

Before we went to school, we came to some knowledge by having faith in people like our parents, relatives, and friends and believing what they told us about our world. When we went to school, we had faith in our teachers and believed what they told us and what we learned from the textbooks and library books. Even in doing experiments in chemistry, we had faith in the teacher or the person who wrote the workbook and thus were willing to believe the directions for experiments given by the teacher or workbook. And even then, do we not have to have faith in what we see actually happening in the experiments?

We had faith in and believed the people who told us about how to apply for a grant for college or how to apply for a job or work for a career. Indeed, it was our experience that validated—up to a point—the things we were told. But it was our faith that moved us into the experience in the first place.

Faith is somewhat like the rocket stages of a space shuttle that propels the shuttle into orbit. These rocket stages eventually get scuttled when no longer needed. But being scuttled should not diminish their value in our understanding of how the space shuttle got to space in the first place. Belief and faith are critical to human experience or else we would not come to much knowledge at all, and what knowledge we would acquire would be very limited. Then, once we attain knowledge with the degree of certainty it brings, faith has a needed tendency to hang around to keep us trusting the knowledge we have acquired and to keep our minds open to growth and change in regard to the facts that support that knowledge.

So much of this aspect of the ability and need to believe and have faith has gotten lost in the time of the Age of Enlightenment. Spurred on by the Industrial Revolution, the proponents of the Enlightenment—in their excitement about the growth of knowledge—downplayed or outright dismissed the need and value of faith. For some, only empirical knowledge had value (i.e., reality that can be experienced and proven).

Obviously, this had a huge effect on matters of religion and, to a large extent, set religion and science needlessly at cross-purposes—both sides being at fault. Only in recent times has there been somewhat of a better understanding and mutual respect between these two fields. However, in the present age of technology and science, our need and ability to have faith is not readily noticed or even recognized. Ironically, it is needed more than ever.

When it comes to knowledge and to understanding the human spirit, belief and faith are absolutely critical. It is then that *believing leads to sight*. Then the saying becomes *I'll see it when I believe it*. A simple example will show what I mean. Just as *get real!* is a response we hear, often, *prove it!* is another. Even in the mathematical and philosophical world of QEDs,[1] faith and the willingness to believe are necessary partners. The journey from proposition to demonstration demands various acts of basic faith and trust. I have to trust that the mathematical symbols have a certain value and maintain that same value throughout the demonstration. I have to trust my sight that what I am seeing is actually what is there. We take these human acts of believing for granted and include them in the proof. But the proof is held together for us by our believing, accepting, and applying these mathematical and philosophical concepts.

Try to prove that you love someone. We work hard at this all the time without giving too much thought to it. We try to be nice. We try to be helpful and caring. And most of the time our acts have good results. We get along with people, and they recognize our good efforts. Then there are those times that, no matter what we do, others do not appreciate our efforts. Recall something of your teenage years when you felt awkward and perhaps thought that no one cared. Maybe you didn't particularly feel loved. In this example, we can come to an understanding of the importance of *faith* in the *love* dynamic. No one can prove love to another person unless that person really has faith or believes that at some level he or she is lovable. If people do not love themselves, they are unlikely to actually recognize love or allow themselves to be vulnerable enough to be loved by another. On the other hand, if they do have a healthy love of self, they will recognize and accept the caring actions of others as signs of love for them.

As we live our life and trust that belief will lead us to faith and to a greater knowledge of ourselves, we find out that there is more to us than meets the eye. Besides love, there are other spiritual qualities in the world that enrich our lives even more than any material good. Michael Leach—quoting the psychiatrist, Dr. Thomas Hora, in *The National Catholic Reporter* column, "Soul Searching,"[2]—explains that we can see honesty; we can see integrity; we can see beauty; we can see love; we can see goodness; we can see joy; we can see peace; we can see harmony; and we can see intelligence. None of these things have any form; none of these things can be imagined; none of these things is tangible; and yet they can be seen. There are also different degrees of qualities like honesty, integrity, and beauty. So by what organ or faculty do people see these invisible things? Some people call it the soul, spirit, or consciousness. We are spiritual beings endowed with spiritual faculties of perception.

We know that people can perform the same external act but for totally different reasons and/or purposes. Jesus spoke to this when he said, "When you give alms, do not let your left hand know what your right hand is doing...when you pray, go to your inner room...when you fast, anoint your head and wash your face, and do not look gloomy." Jesus is saying we should not be doing these things to be seen or praised but to be sincere.

The purpose of these reflections is to come to an understanding of the importance of belief and faith in our life in general so that, when it comes to our *spirit life,* we will come to recognize and value belief and faith as a necessary part of our growth and maturity.

Father Richard Rohr explains the substance of the faith-knowledge tension.

> *As long as we can deal with life in universal abstractions, we can pretend that the usual binary (black or white; physical or spiritual; right or wrong) way of thinking is true, but once we deal with a specific or concrete reality, it is always, without exception, a mixture of darkness and light, death and life, good and bad, attractive and unattractive.*[3]

He goes on to say that our *black and white, physical or spiritual, right or wrong* mentality has a difficult time holding things in creative tension. It actually confuses rigid thinking, or black-and-white thinking, with faith itself. Faith is exactly the opposite—which is precisely why we call it "faith" and not logic.

The *divine becoming human* must always show itself in the specific, the concrete, the particular (as in Jesus), and it always refuses to be a mere abstraction.

> *If nature abhors a vacuum, Christ abhors a vagueness. If God is love, Christ is love for this one person, this one place, this one time-bound and time-ravaged self.*[4]

There is a story of a little girl eating at her friend's house. Her friend's mother asks her if she likes brussels sprouts. "Yes, of course I like brussels sprouts," the little girl replies. After dinner the mother notices that her little guest has not eaten a single sprout. "I thought you liked brussels sprouts," the mother says. The little girl answered, "Oh, I do, but not enough to actually eat them."

It's fairly easy to hang out with big universal ideas and argue about theory. It is easy to think that I love humankind, just not some individual persons.

> *The universal usually just gives us a way out. The concrete gives us a way in.*[5]

Like the little girl and brussels sprouts, it is equally easy to like what Christ says and teaches—but not enough to actually put what he says and teaches into action. To do that, we have to "get real!"—or as Sherlock Holmes might respond, "Faith...elementary my dear Christian Watson."

And if the *divine becoming human* must always show itself in the specific, the concrete, the particular…we will come to see the sacraments as important specific, concrete, and particular *faith signs* of the love and care that God—through the family of faith—has for us…as well as the love and care we must have for them and, through them, for God. So that is why I see reflecting on the individual sacraments a natural corollary to the reflection on faith. The sacraments can position us in life to help us recognize and remember some of the significant ways that continue God's incarnational plan and blessings of redemption as Paul proclaimed in his letter to the Ephesians in chapter 1 of the book by that name, verses 1 through 23.

> *Blessed be the God and Father of our Lord Jesus Christ, who has blessed us with every spiritual blessing in the heavenly places in Christ, just as [God] chose us in [Christ] before the foundation of the world, that we would be holy and blameless before Him. In love [God] predestined us to adoption as [children] through Jesus Christ to Himself…In [Christ] we have redemption through His blood, the forgiveness of our trespasses…In all wisdom and insight [God] made known to us the mystery of His will…*(Ephesians 1:3–8).

"However, when the Son of Man comes, will he find faith on the earth?" (Luke 18:8). This quote is Jesus's seemingly rhetorical question after telling his disciples the parable about the necessity for them to pray without becoming weary. Is the plan and blessings of redemption that Paul announced possible in our world and in our life? We will never know unless we have the faith to actually begin to live according to the plan and to be open to receive the redemptive blessings. Like fish that swim in an ocean without awareness, humans swim in an ocean of faith—many without awareness.

Unless our faith is strong, we will miss so much of what life has to offer. And what a tragedy that would be!

Chapter One

∞A Life Open to Believing∞

We know everything today and believe almost nothing...But what [we] believe is what [we] pay attention to, what [we] care about, what finally lives and matters in [us]...It is not what [we] know that matters, it is what [we] believe—and believe all the way through.[6] —Richard Rohr

The power of believing

Our ability to believe is one of the greatest powers we have. No one can force another to believe anything. Only individuals themselves can commit themselves to believe something. Fear or threat of force can be exerted on people to force compliance, but that does not take away the freedom or ability to believe otherwise. It is a great pathology not to be able to engage one's ability to believe. That pathology can lead easily to major anxiety and despair.

Viktor Frankl, an Austrian neurologist and psychologist as well as a Holocaust survivor, speaks to this power of believing. Trying to come to some understanding as to why some prisoners survived while others did not, he illustrates in his book *Man's Search for Meaning*[7] this ability to believe even in the terrible circumstances of a concentration camp. He, himself, spent three years in various concentration camps, including Theresienstadt, Auschwitz, and Dachau.

Quoting Nietzsche, "Those who have a 'why' to live, can bear with almost any 'how.'" He remembers those who walked through the huts comforting others, giving away their last piece of bread. "They may have been few in number," he said, "but they offer sufficient proof that everything can be taken from a [person] but one thing: the last of the human freedoms—to choose one's attitude in any sort of circumstances, to choose one's own way."[8] And then he says, "Forces beyond your control can take away everything you possess except one thing: your freedom to choose how you will respond to the situation."[9]

He then reflected that, given the reality of their circumstances, it did not matter what they expected from life but, rather, what life expected from them. They needed to stop asking about the meaning of life and instead to think of themselves as those who were being questioned by life. "Our answer," he said, "must consist, not in talk and meditation, but in right action and in right conduct. Life ultimately means taking responsibility to find the right answer to its problems and to fulfill the tasks which it constantly sets for each individual."[10]

Self-constructed obstacles

If that liberating mind-set can happen in the circumstances and experience of a concentration camp, think of what a force it can be outside the barbed wire and the watchtowers. Perhaps we have too great an expectation of what we think knowledge alone can accomplish. We have tended to give knowledge the place of honor as well as a power it does not have. Knowledge cannot sustain itself for long without belief and a will to find meaning. It is imperative to the life of the human spirit that we recognize the place and power of believing if we are going to engage life in search of meaning.

Theresienstadt, Auschwitz, and Dachau are just bad memories now. We are decades removed from those atrocities, and there are some people who deny that they ever happened. Others work very hard to keep the memory alive so that they never happen again. It remains a wonder that people survived such inhuman treatment at the hands of others—denied the basic freedoms and subjected to inhuman conditions. And yet the irony in all of this is what some humans tend to do when they experience personal freedom. Individually, many construct their own personal camps of confinement and torture. Addictive, aggressive, depressive, and self-destructive behavior has reached epidemic levels in Western culture. Frankl sees this as related to the mass phenomenon of the feeling of meaninglessness. *People have enough to live by, but nothing to live for.*[11] People take their freedoms seriously but, more often, individually rather than communally. But even whole cultures and societies tend to use their freedoms to separate rather than unite. Many people opt for the *license to carry* or *stand and defend* rather than the *unity and wisdom to care enough to find a better way*. Many in our society are just angry or fearful; they choose partisanship rather than citizenship and expediency rather than fairness. So many issues seem to become a battleground with little or no room for compromise. All of this addictive, aggressive, depressive, and self-destructive behavior begets a pathology of global proportions resulting in a paralysis of the human spirit. And so we have created and interned ourselves in our own personal camps of *unfreedom*.

It is the *will to meaning* that Frankl came to see as the necessary task to which each person must address him or herself if we are to answer the questions that life asks of us. Frankl sees this *will to meaning* as the primary motivational force in a person instead of the Freudian *will to pleasure* or Adlerian *will to power.*[12] Rabbi Harold Kushner underscores that statement when he says in the foreword of the 2006 edition of Frankl's book that life is not primarily a quest for pleasure, as Freud believed, or a quest for power, as Adler taught, but a quest for meaning.[13]

To embrace the *will to meaning* when our life is going well is one thing. To do so when life becomes difficult or confronts us with suffering is quite another matter. It is our ability to believe that life is meaningful that can sustain us when we are confronted with life's many challenges.

Even if we are the cause of our own suffering, we can tap into the power of the *will to meaning* to deal with life's challenges. Those familiar with the Twelve Steps of Alcoholics Anonymous know that the first three steps state the following:

> 1. *We admitted we were powerless over alcohol—that our lives had become unmanageable.*
>
> 2. *Came to believe that a Power greater than ourselves could restore us to sanity.*
>
> 3. *Made a decision to turn our will and our lives over to the care of God, as we understood Him.*[14]

But we can substitute any of our self-inflicted addiction into this process. What often happens is that the *will to pleasure* or the *will to power* can take over our lives without being properly challenged and questioned as to any purpose or meaning outside themselves. In and of themselves, there is nothing wrong with pleasure and power as long as they don't become the masters of our lives.

Learning to find and give meaning

One of the more frequently used quotes to encourage youth in their struggle with life is "you can be whatever you want to be if you try hard enough." Athletes, politicians, and other professionals repeat this quote quite often when asked about their success. Spoken from the vantage point of holding a trophy or gold medal or having just won an election or having achieved a sought-after goal, it is a statement that can be a source of encouragement for those listening. And there is a lot of truth in what is said.

Hidden in and underlying the statement, however, is the reality of the doubts, the disappointments, and the pain that accompanied those individual journeys. And at each doubt, each disappointment, and every pain, the individual had to grow in his or her ability to believe, and that carried the person to the next step. Nor can we ignore the reality that there are other factors and that no matter how much people may want something or how hard they try, they may not achieve their goal. But given these disclaimers, the quote is an encouraging one because it is open ended and thus gives individuals encouraging space to apply their talent and motivation.

Frankl[15] cites a survey that John Hopkins University conducted among almost eight thousand students from forty-eight colleges asking them what they considered very important to them now. Sixteen percent checked "making a lot of money." Seventy-eight percent checked "finding a purpose and meaning in my life." And sometimes that purpose and meaning comes to us from unexpected places and in surprising ways. Such is the truth of this prayer that an anonymous Confederate soldier wrote.

> *I asked God for strength that I might achieve.*
> *I was made weak that I might learn humbly to obey.*
> *I asked for health that I might do greater things.*
> *I was given infirmity that I might do better things.*
> *I asked for riches that I might be happy.*
> *I was given poverty that I might be wise.*
> *I asked for power that I might have the praise of men.*
> *I was given weakness that I might feel the need of God.*
> *I asked for all things that I might enjoy life.*
> *I was given life that I might enjoy all things.*
> *I got nothing that I asked for, but everything I hoped for.*

*Almost despite myself, my unspoken prayers
were answered.
I am, among all [people], most richly blessed.*

Only one's ability to believe and trust can sustain the human spirit in such a transformation and awareness. Sister Ruth Barrows, O. Carm., has put this issue of faith and the very real need to take it seriously in perspective as she writes in her book *Essence of Prayer*[16] that it was her experience that faith does not get the attention it ought to have. Too often people take it for granted that they have faith and that they live by faith. No doubt this is true in an overall sort of way. But faith, to be real faith, is incessant: always operating, governing the entirety of life with nothing whatever left out, governing thinking, points of view, the forming of judgments, and actions. This is impossible without enormous, specific attention. Our natural, spontaneous way of acting…is to live by what our feelings tell us is the truth of things…and we just assume this is the reality.

Feelings and emotions certainly enrich our lives, but if we live just by what our feelings and emotions tell us, the truth would be changing in an almost constant flux while at the same time enclosing us in a very narrow space—much like a hamster running its wheel in its cage.

Faith on the other hand, because it is open ended and ongoing, empowers us to engage life in all the ways it unfolds before us. It is this openness and encouragement regarding faith and the Kingdom of God that seems to be the hallmark of the teachings of Jesus.

I use the term *Kingdom of God* because Jesus did. Sandra M. Schneiders, IHM,[17] explains that while many contemporary Christians prefer *Reign of God* or *Kindom* because it is less patriarchal then *Kingdom,* Jesus used the word *kingdom* for a reason. By calling the reality he had been sent to inaugurate a *kingdom*—since there could not be two different kingdoms in operation in the same place and same time—he was invalidating the violent [rule] of the Romans. He was inviting his hearers to live in a new kingdom structured by inclusive, compassionate love and justice—a kingdom where only God is sovereign.

And so Jesus put before them another parable:

> *The Kingdom of Heaven is like a mustard seed that someone took and sowed in his field; it is the smallest of all the seeds, but when it has grown it is the greatest of shrubs and becomes a tree, so that the birds of the air come and make nests in its branches.*[18]

The beauty of this short parable is how packed it is with meaning. It isn't just about a small seed growing into a great shrub and therefore becoming something of value. The greatness begins in the smallness of the seed itself and the fact that it has within itself the potential—the very blueprint itself— of what it takes to become a great shrub. Obviously, all the seeds do not realize their potential for a variety of reasons. Jesus gives us the parable of the sower and the seeds as an example of what can and does happen.[19]

On the one hand, we can marvel at the seed and it smallness. But we cannot make its smallness the end of our admiration. We have to give it time so that it can grow. We must also marvel at its growth. And we marvel at the fact that the birds of the air have found a home in it (and probably have eaten some of its seeds, but Jesus doesn't go there). What Jesus is teaching his disciples and us about is the dynamic of faith and the Kingdom of God. Both are living and therefore vibrant and growing. And therein lies something of a stumbling block in our

19

coming to know and understand the Kingdom of God. It is like the difference between a still-life picture and a motion picture.

The parables of Jesus—Still-life and motion pictures

A *still life* gives us time to concentrate and study the image. A *motion* picture is a series of *still-life* pictures that carries us along with the various images. Both are authentic ways to learn and discover. Both have their positive and negative sides. Together they complement each other and present a more complete understanding. We need the power of both to appreciate what Jesus is trying to teach us.

For example, the following is a teaching of Jesus:

Occasions for stumbling are bound to come, but woe to anyone by whom they come! It would be better for you if a millstone were hung around your neck and you were thrown into the sea than for you to cause one of these little ones to stumble. Be on your guard! If another disciple sins, you must rebuke the offender, and if there is repentance, you must forgive. And if the same person sins against you seven times a day, and turns back to you seven times and says, "I repent," you must forgive.[20]

As a *still life*, this is a difficult teaching even for the apostles. So Luke tells us (and only Luke records this) that they had a tough time with this saying. The apostles said to the Lord, "Increase our faith!"

The Lord replied, *If you had the faith the size of a mustard seed, you could say to this mulberry tree, 'Be uprooted and planted in the sea,' and it would obey you.* (Matthew 18:6-9; Mark 9:42-48 and Luke 17:1-6)

Jesus did not water down his parable or say that he didn't mean it or that they didn't understand him. He did mean it, and they did understand it. They just did not think they were capable of living it. So Jesus encourages them by saying that they, and we, have the seed of faith necessary to make this happen—not the uprooting of mulberry trees but the need to forgive, and we need to grow into it. Faith is our gift-seed; its power source is the Holy Spirit, and its soil is our life.

The greatest detriment to faith

There is a tendency to limit the meaning of faith to a code of ethics or creed. Faith is not a thing. It is primarily the dynamic way we relate to people, places, and things, and its importance is related to how we use its potential. The greatest detriment to faith and the greatest sin[21] is trying to limit what we believe the Spirit can accomplish in us and where the Spirit wishes to lead us. This is true for the individual Christian as well as the entire Christian community.

This truth is played out like a motion picture in the book of Acts[22] where we have the story about Cornelius, Peter, and the working of the Spirit in the early Christian community. Cornelius is a centurion of the Italian Cohort—a Roman soldier and a Gentile. Luke tells us that Cornelius and his household were devout people who feared God. Cornelius experiences a vision in which he is told by an angel of God that his prayers and almsgiving "have ascended as a memorial before God." He is instructed to send representatives to Joppa and seek a certain "Simon," also called "Peter."

The story scene shifts to Joppa, and we are told that the next day Peter went to the roof to pray. There, Peter has a vision of various animals (clean and unclean according to Jewish custom) lowered from the sky on a huge sheet. The voice of the Lord tells him, "Get up, kill, and eat!" Peter responds that he has never eaten anything profane or unclean. The Voice responds,

"What God has made clean, you must not call profane." With Peter it seems like everything happens in threes because he has the same dream three times before the sheet was taken back to heaven.

What is interesting in these encounters is the way that God chooses to move both Cornelius and Peter to deeper faith. Cornelius and his whole household are people of faith. The angel acknowledges this in saying, "Your prayers and your alms have ascended as a memorial before God." The angel then instructs Cornelius to send for this certain Simon, who is called Peter. And so Cornelius does as the angel says; he sends for Peter.

In the meantime, God is bringing Simon Peter to deeper faith by pointing out to him what God considers *clean*. At one level Peter knows what is clean and unclean. He is about to be taken to a whole new level of understanding and seeing as God sees and understands. *What God has made clean, you must not call profane.*

The Spirit and the faith of Cornelius and Peter

The visions, which both Cornelius and Peter experience, prepare them for the movement of the Spirit in them and, through them, in the church. Cornelius, obviously a person of deep faith as his prayers and actions ascend as "a memorial before God," is led by the Spirit to a deeper understanding of the faith that he has, but now it will grow within the Christian community represented by the person of Peter. The church, in and through Peter, is led by the Spirit to a deeper and broader understanding of the faith that it embraces as it experiences the movement of the Spirit in the non-Jewish and non-Christian household of Cornelius.

We see this reflected as the story continues. Peter is trying to make sense of the vision when the servants sent by

Cornelius arrive. The *voice* of the Spirit nudges Peter to get up and meet the messengers at the door. They present their credentials and relay Cornelius's message: that he was directed by the holy angel to send for Peter to come to his house and to hear what he had to say.

When they arrive at the house, Cornelius had already gathered together his relatives and close friends—all Gentiles. Peter enters the house with the disclaimer, "You yourselves know that it is unlawful for a Jew to associate with or to visit a Gentile, but the Lord has shown me that I should not call anyone profane or unclean." Peter saw clearly the connection between his vision and the present moment.

Then it seems the Spirit of God clearly affirms the visions of both Cornelius and Peter. Luke tells us that "while Peter was still speaking, the Holy Spirit fell upon all who heard the word." And the Jewish believers who accompanied Peter were astonished "that the gift of the Holy Spirit had been poured out on the Gentiles."[23]

What the Pentecostal Spirit of God accomplished in the upper room through the apostles, the Spirit of God was accomplishing in the house of Gentiles. "Can anyone withhold the water for baptizing these people who have received the Holy Spirit just as we have?" And so we have another Pentecost when the wind of the Spirit blows where the Spirit wills.

The Spirit and the faith of the church

But the story doesn't end there. As we read in the very next chapter of the Acts of the Apostles, members of the church in Jerusalem confronted Peter: "You entered the house of the uncircumcised and ate with them."[24] Peter then relates to them what he experienced in the vision on the roof and what happened in the house of Cornelius and how "...the Holy Spirit fell upon them as it had upon us at the beginning...If then God gave them the same gift that he gave us when we believed in the Lord Jesus Christ, who was I to be able to hinder God?"

What a tragedy it would have been if Peter had chosen to limit himself and the church to the faith as he understood it because it was what he knew, and it was safe. His experience of Jesus dealing with the Pharisees (the Sabbath was made for humankind and not humankind for the Sabbath[25]) convinced him that he must force himself to be open to the Spirit if he was to prove his love and follow Christ: "feed my [Jesus's] sheep!"[26]

The Spirit and the faith of believers

We must all be open to this Advocate promised by Jesus and sent by the Father: "If in my name you ask me for anything, I will do it. If you love me, you will keep my commandments. And I will ask the Father, and he will give you another Advocate, to be with you forever. This is the Spirit of truth, whom the world cannot receive, because it neither sees him nor knows him."[27] We must be open to all the ways the Spirit chooses to lead us and not just the ways that fall within our comfort zone.

Pope Benedict XVI proclaimed a *Year of Faith* on October 11, 2011, to begin October 11, 2012, and to end November 24, 2013. During this time the people of God were called to a *New Evangelization*, which summons us to *an authentic and renewed conversion to the Lord. Conversion* because we, like the disciples, have ignored or misunderstood the direction the Spirit has been leading; *authentic* because this conversion is empowered by the Spirit; *renewed* because we have lost something of our ability to hear what the Spirit is revealing.

This New Evangelization is directed firstly and foremost to the individual Catholic. This embracing of the good news revealed in and through Jesus, God's Anointed One, takes place not in foreign territory but in the homeland of each

Christian soul. Its purpose is to allow the Gospel to reclaim us—
so that we, who have been created in the image and likeness
of God, really believe and act like we are children of God; so
that we, who have been redeemed by the life, suffering, death,
and resurrection of Jesus, God's Anointed One, will live like we
have been redeemed and forgiven; and so that we, who have
been promised the gift of advocacy in the very Spirit of God, will
be open so that the Spirit can advocate in our lives. It is this
openness in faith to the Spirit that engages us in a *special and
specific* way through our life and, then and only then, through
the way we relate to the world and all who inhabit it.

The dynamic spirit of faith

This *special and specific way* of faith is the way of love.
It is the basis for all that Jesus taught. *Love* is perhaps the most
commonly used word and theme in songs and poetry. It is the
most sought-after emotional and spiritual experience. And yet it
defies our attempts to define it, quantify it, understand it, and—
least of all—contain it. *Love* is what it is, and we will see it only
when we believe enough to embrace it as a way of living. Quite
the opposite of the adage "seeing is believing," we need to
believe so that we can see. When it comes to love, we must
believe before we can even start to see. And then we never
actually physically see love itself. We only see expressions and
mosaic pieces of what we believe is love.

A child asks a parent, "How much do you love me?" The
parent spreads his or her arms as wide as possible, encircles
the child, squeezes, and says, "This much and more." The child
giggles with joy. The joy comes because the child believes
himself or herself to be lovable. What is true of the child is true
of all of us. In one way or the other, we are always searching
for signs of love or indicators of our worth. Once we believe we
are lovable, then and only then will we risk loving others. And

that is precisely why Jesus focused so strongly on the fact that God first loved us without condition and without limit.

It is difficult for us to understand *without condition and without limit* and yet that is the deep yearning in our hearts. We desire it, but we find it almost impossible—if not impossible—to think we can give it. That is why we have to allow the Spirit to help us grow into it—step by step, day by day, and moment by moment. It must become our mustard-seed experience.

Signs of this dynamic Spirit

That is why Jesus promised to send the Spirit to be our Advocate, our guide, so that we can grow into the fullness of faith. Jesus says,

> *I still have many things to say to you, but you cannot bear them now. When the Spirit of truth comes, he will guide you into all the truth; for he will not speak on his own, but will speak whatever he hears, and he will declare to you the things that are to come* (John 16:12–13).

Within the Roman Catholic faith, that step-by-step, day-by-day, moment-by-moment growth is formed and nourished in living the sacramental life. The sacraments give our spirits the soil to grow in our relationship to God, our Creator, Redeemer, and Sanctifier. The sacraments are not simply abstract religious rituals disconnected from our daily lives; rather, they mirror the dynamics of our human life experience: being born—baptism; maturing in spirit—confirmation; growing—nourished by the Body and Blood of Jesus, Eucharist (Holy Communion); forgiving and being forgiven—reconciliation; living a chosen way, fulfilling the original blessing of God to increase and multiply—marriage; and fulfilling the command of Jesus to make disciples of all nations in and through the call of the church—sacred orders; and finally, being borne away by sickness and death—holy anointing.

Here again, we can look at these experiences as *still-life* pictures or *ongoing and moving* pictures. For example, there is the moment of birth, but it is a moment that bespeaks many life moments that have already come before and many life moments that will come after birth. Being born is hardly the beginning, and it certainly is not the end of a person's life. It is a step and a moment opening into an unknown future.

So it is with the sacramental faith life of a person. If there is to be a *new evangelization* and if it is to be successful, it will have to happen with openness to the *movement* and *moving* Spirit of God and all the ways in which the Spirit of God chooses to reveal truth.

The truth is this: that God embraces us with love. Each one of the sacraments conveys within itself the ongoing, providential, and *divine-becoming-flesh* love that God has for us. It is this love that makes each sacrament open ended. By this I mean that although the sacraments begin in time and are lived in time, they point through time to an eternal reality beyond time—namely, the Kingdom of God's Love.

So at baptism we are recognized and named as a child of God, thus given an identity that we will carry throughout our earthly life into eternity. Confirmation seals our being inspirited by the Holy Spirit. Eucharist gathers us and nourishes us as the People of God. Marriage seals the love-covenant of the couple shepherding the home and exemplifying the love-covenant of God. Holy Orders seals the love-covenant of the ordained shepherding the church and exemplifying the shepherding love of God. Reconciliation and the anointing of the sick sustain and move us through an imperfect world toward a restoring of original innocence in our spirit and a body made whole by our resurrection.

Dying is not the worst tragedy that can happen to us;
living without faith is a far greater tragedy.

± Bringing the Faith to Life ±

The purpose of parables and sacraments

It is toward this openness and unlimited dimension of the sacraments that the following reflections are offered. I believe that what is true of the Spirit—namely, that the greatest detriment to faith, and the greatest sin, is trying to limit what the Spirit can accomplish in us and where the Spirit wishes to lead us—is also true of the sacraments. This happens because, in the human endeavor to understand something, we try to fit it into a preconceived and limited human context. That is understandable, and certainly Jesus was fully aware of this human limitation. That is why he taught the way he did. He taught in parables.

Parables are stories that are open ended. Jesus would draw the listeners into a story setting that seemed comfortable. When the listeners became engrossed, he invited them to a new view–a new way to look at a truth. For example, when a lawyer asks Jesus who his neighbor is,[14] Jesus replies with the parable where a traveler falls victim to robbers. After being passed by a couple of times, a Samaritan comes along, gets close, and helps the victim—even to the point of taking him to a place to stay and recover. Then Jesus asks the lawyer whom he thinks was neighbor to the victim. Obviously, it is the one who helped him. "Go and do likewise," Jesus says.

The story line is pretty straightforward. But there is much more to all of this. As we begin to read this passage of the Gospel of Luke, we see that Jesus is engaging the disciples with the understanding that they are blessed because of what they are seeing and hearing. Whether they actually were coming to that understanding or not, we do not know. Perhaps it was in preparation for what was about to happen. What was to follow is the story of the lawyer testing Jesus about what he thought was the greatest commandment, followed by the parable of the Good Samaritan.

Having heard the story so many times in our lives, we easily come down on the side of Jesus and take some delight in his confounding the lawyer. However, we have no emotional, cultural, or political resources or agendas involved. We see the Samaritan as good because we know the end of the story. Had we started listening with the same emotional, cultural, and political baggage as the lawyer, the ending would be much more troubling—not only for the lawyer, but also for the disciples who may not have seen themselves as being so blessed in having to face the decision to "go and do likewise" in their life.

Let us imagine that Jesus told the parable today in Israel, and it was a Palestinian who offered help; or in Syria, where it was an Israeli; or in the United States, where it was an Iranian; or in Iran, where it was an American. Then the baggage that people might bring to those stories would perhaps be more real today than the ancient issues of Jews and Samaritans.

But to really understand the impact of the parable, Jesus wants us to take this parable as personally as possible so that it can take us beyond our dislikes, our prejudices, and our judgments of others. With the help of the Spirit, we can begin to see neighbors where before we only saw the competitor or the enemy—that is, if we dared to look at them at all. To believe in Jesus is relatively harmless; making his beliefs our beliefs is what really can create problems for us. And being *in* the world but not *of* the world can be confusing for us. That is why we have the Gift of the Spirit to strengthen us in our discernment as to whether or not we choose to "go and do likewise."[28]

The Reverend Billy Graham has written a book of reflections entitled *Hope for Each Day*. In his entry for September 16 he writes this:

> *A boat doesn't sink because it is in the water. It sinks because the water gets into it. In the same way, Christians don't fail to live as they should because they are in the world; they fail because the world has gotten into them. We don't fail to produce the fruit of the Holy Spirit because we live in a sea of corruption; we fail because the sea of corruption has gotten into us.*[29]

That is why we have been given the sacraments, which strengthen us in our day-to-day deciding of whether or not to "go and do likewise." The sacraments are not rewards for being good nor are they, as Cardinal Martini noted, *a disciplinary instrument.* They are meant to be a help to people at times on their journey when they are in need of new strength. They help us to live and view the world in loving and caring ways. They help us to avoid the world getting so deeply into us that we lose sight of who we are and who God is in our life. So let us see what the sacraments have to offer by way of strength, encouragement, and discernment in our "going and doing," as Jesus invites us to do.

The purpose of ritual

We hear and do the same thing over and over. This can be the common lament of churchgoers routinely bored in the pews. And these are not just the children and teenagers. Adults who have been going to church for years can also be confounded by the need for ritual, especially if it doesn't seem to change much or catch our attention or isn't artfully performed or entertaining. Why do we do it over and over?

The main reason is that *ritual can help make us strong in mind when our memory grows weak.* Anyone growing up in the

1940s, '50s, or '60s might remember the pageantry of Memorial Day with its ritual of parades, music, red carnations, and speeches. The purpose was to honor those who sacrificed, suffered, or died to keep our country and our world free. Communities gathered to celebrate. Local high-school bands played and marched. Veterans paraded wearing their uniforms and carrying flags. Each year it was basically the same, but with new faces as well as aging faces. The ritual was meant to proclaim the message of, and help us realize, the price of our freedom and the sacrifices made. But the farther distant the collective memory got, the more it faded. The veterans got older and died, fewer people came out, and fewer bands played. There are still a few expressions of remembrance, but it no longer holds the attention of the collective memory of the nation. It is not a ritual issue; it is a memory issue. But there are rituals that have remained the same for decades and have thrived.

Every year there is the thoroughbred horse race for the Triple Crown. There is the Kentucky Derby, the Preakness, and the Belmont Stakes. Each race has the same ritual for the most part. There is the call for *riders up*, the walk around the paddock, the walk through the tunnel to the track, and the trumpet call to the gate. Each venue has its proper song—"My Old Kentucky Home"; "Maryland, My Maryland"; "New York, New York"—and then there is the parade up and down the track, the walk to the starting gate, and finally the starting bell. The ritual described adds up to anywhere from twenty to thirty minutes. The race itself varies somewhat, depending on conditions, but averages a total of less than seven minutes for all three races. What makes certain rituals successful is that people prepare and bring meaning and memory to the events.

Even simple rituals like high-school athletes putting on their uniforms in a particular order or not washing them after a victory speaks to the importance one places on a ritual, even if a bit superstitious. Whether or not a particular rite is meaningful has a lot to do with what a person remembers to bring to it.

In life, culture, family, or faith traditions, the younger generation, in many ways, is dependent on the older generation to pass along the meaning they attach to a particular ritual or custom. Just doing something doesn't impress unless the *why* or the *meaning* is given. And even then it may not be enough for the younger generation that has not had the experience of the older generation. That is why ritual requires three things to happen to establish meaning: *preparation, the event, and the reflection* out of which can develop a personal and, hopefully, meaningful experience for the younger generation.

Superficial reasons can hold people to a ritual for a short time. Family reunions that involve two or more generations draw members who come because mom and dad brought them as children, told them they had to come as young teens, and let them make the decision as older teens. Hopefully, some meaningful relationships with cousins, grandparents, uncles, and aunts keep them coming back as often as possible. Older members keep coming because they have experienced something important in this kind of personal contact, so extra effort is made to be there. Experiencing something important in this kind of personal contact becomes the bedrock for keeping the ritual of family reunions alive.

The purpose of sacramental rituals

The human dynamic by which *ritual can help make us stronger in mind when our memory grows weak* is important if we are to understand the sacraments and the empowerment they are meant to bring us. Each of the sacraments raises a specific memory that can bring the gift of meaning to our lives.

The *Sacrament of Baptism* reminds us that we are each a child of God. It reminds the faith community of the privilege and responsibility to lead the one baptized into this understanding and experience of being a child of God.

The *Sacrament of Confirmation* reminds us of Jesus's promise to send the Holy Spirit. The sacrament imparts the gifts of the Holy Spirit on those confirmed, as well as reminds the faith community of the privilege and responsibility to help those who are confirmed to be open to the Holy Spirit, to understand that the Holy Spirit is present in the community, and to recognize the gifts and fruits that signal the Holy Spirit's presence there (in the community) and in one's life.

The *Sacrament of Eucharist* is the center of remembrance. It was when doing the celebration of the Passover—the Jewish ritual meal of remembering the Lord delivering the people from slavery and leading them to freedom—that Jesus gave us a new and eternal covenant. In the breaking of bread and the sharing of the cup, Jesus gave us the *do this in remembrance of me* invitation—not only for remembering his body and blood poured out for us but to remind us of our own becoming his very body and blood poured out for the world.

When we forget that we are a child of God empowered by the Spirit and that we are the Body of Christ, we know that we lose focus, and our behavior gives evidence to this forgetting. And so the *Sacrament of Reconciliation* is our bridge to re-membering ourselves to the Body of Christ. It helps us to correct our out-of-focus vision of God, ourselves, those around us, and creation. We easily forget that we are children of adoption, not children of entitlement. So when we step out of line, we need to open ourselves to the loving forgiveness of God.

It is in the environment of the human family that the sacraments are celebrated and brought to life. So the *Sacrament of the Anointing of the Sick* reminds us that we are mortal and fragile, and we need a remedy to help us deal with life when it challenges our mortality. It sustains us in redeeming our life even as we suffer. It helps us remember that there is meaning in our mortal life even as we let go of it in the hope of eternal life.

The *Sacrament of Marriage* expresses a *Covenant of Love* that shepherds the home and family. It reminds us that marriage is a covenant: not a contract, not a quid pro quo, not "I will love you *if…*or *as long as…*" The model for such a covenant of love is God's commitment of love for all of us. It is absolute and unconditional. The grace of this sacrament is to help the couple grow ever more strongly into such a covenant so that together they give witness to God's love and care to those around them.

The *Sacrament of Holy Orders* expresses a *Covenant of Love* that shepherds the family of faith. As in marriage, the model for such a covenant of love is God's commitment of love. The grace of this sacrament is to help those ordained grow ever more strongly into such a covenant so that they proclaim and give sacramental witness to God's love and care for all of the people of God.

All the sacraments above are reminders of Jesus Christ who is the One Sacrament of God's love. "For God so loved the world that he gave his only Son, so that everyone who believes in him may not perish but may have eternal life."[30]

Chapter Two

∞The Sacraments of Initiation∞

Difficulty' is the name of an ancient tool that was created purely to help us define who we are.[31]

—Paulo Coelho

Searching for our identity

From the first moment of our existence, we have an identity—an identity that is always in relationship. All the moments after that, we spend trying to find it. Part of that time we are given an identity: we are the child of so-and-so, brother or sister to others in the family, a relative of some kind to the extended family members, and a genealogy of a long or short line of ancestors. Then as we mature our identity gets more complex as we develop our own personality, attract friends, attach ourselves to people, places, and things, choose and follow a career pattern, and—statistically speaking—most likely marry and have a family. Our identity, although uniquely individual, is always in relationship to someone, something, or some place. We are not just uniquely individual unto ourselves. Even our social-security number, although a unique identifier, is issued to us by others.

Trying to find our identity in the midst of a maze of complex configurations can be distracting, time consuming, and involve running into a lot of dead ends. There are times when we are not so sure we want to be the child, brother, sister, or relative of so-and-so. We change personalities, friends, places, careers, and even spouses over time, which is even more confusing. In the midst of all this, we can lose the foundational footing of our identity and feel absolutely lost in life. We find happiness to be elusive because we do not know whom it is we are trying to make happy.

Hopefully, in our searching there are loving and forgiving people to whom we are related who are there to help us by pointing us in the right direction, reminding us of our roots in family and friends, and giving us the space and time to refind ourselves and the traits that give our identity real value.

But the search for our identity must also have a uniquely spiritual component, without which we will never remotely come close to knowing our true self. Science and technology can give us genealogies, DNA histories, anthropological research, psychological profiles, telescopic and microscopic evidence of our universe—all of which are a true blessing and provide enriching knowledge. This blessing and knowledge of science and technology create in us a wonder and awe of our world and universe. It explains much about *the how* of things working. But questions about *the why* and *the who* are left in the realm of mystery. The science of biology informs us about how a child is conceived and comes to birth and the wonder of it all. But science cannot answer questions about the uniqueness and the depth of identity—namely, who a person is.

Faith in the knowledge of science takes us on an amazing journey as far as it goes. Faith in our ability to believe can take us far beyond the limits and boundaries of space and time. Without an initiation into our physical life by experiences that help us to learn something of our identity, we would have a difficult time establishing an identity for ourselves that didn't have gaps of not knowing.

The same is true of the spiritual dimension of our identity. Being initiated into the spiritual dimension of our lives helps us to come to an understanding of *the why* and *the who* of our being and thus helps us better come to know who we are and why we are. *The why* of our being is happiness and *the who* of our being is God. Like in our physical life, our identity is always relational, so our identity in the spiritual life is always relational. The initiating process of both our physical and spiritual life is birth, growth (maturation), and nourishment. This process in our spiritual lives includes baptism, confirmation, and Eucharist—three sacraments and signs identifying our relationship with God, community, and all humanity.

"In the name of the Father and of the Son and of the Holy Spirit. Amen"

This short prayer can be used to offer praise, intention, and gratitude for what we are about to do or what we are doing or what we have done. It helps to center and connect us to the God who made us, redeemed us, and sanctified us. It puts us in a Trinitarian community of love.

Our faith community initiates us into this Trinitarian community of love with three signs or sacraments. We are rebirthed in the waters of baptism as one who is made in the image and likeness of God, our Creator. Rebirthed as a child of God, our Creator, we receive the Spirit of God's holy gifts in the signing of chrism. Rebirthed as a child of God and gifted by the Holy Spirit, we are sustained, nourished, and redeemed as we partake of the Bread of Life and the cup of salvation in memory of him who lived, died, and rose again.

Much preparation is spent preparing for these sacraments. For the most part, they represent a special time of celebration for the family of faith. For families of those initiated, it is often a reunion time of sorts. Usually it is a time of gift giving and sharing a meal. Baptismal garments might have been handed down for generations. Being chosen as a godparent or sponsor is seen as an honor. It is a time for taking family photos and saving mementos. All of these things are good and help make these times of initiation special. They help identify us and fix these events in our memory.

In the midst of this, we must not forget that although they are *initiating* sacraments, they are also *sustaining* sacraments. *Although the rites themselves have closure, the realities they signify do not.* Baptism, confirmation, and Eucharist are all open ended—always giving birth to a greater life, always confirming the many gifts of the Spirit in deeper and innumerable ways, always sustaining, nourishing, and redeeming our life in the divine community of love.

± Bringing the Rite to Life ±

Symbols—perhaps a class ring or clothes with the logo of our favorite sports team or a souvenir of place that we visited—are important as they remind us of important moments in our life or common connections with other people. Refrigerators in homes with children have all kinds of memorabilia, along with calendars of upcoming events to remind us of loved ones and schedules.

Sacramental rites have many symbols that can help us to engage their *sustaining* power long after we receive them. But we must know them, remember them, and use them with some sense of regularity for them to be helpful. In the regular course of things, we keep photos of significant loved ones readily available. We see them often. Then there are other things like class yearbooks and albums that can either get lost in closets or routinely be brought out and enjoyed.

After each section on a sacrament, there will be a reflection, "Bringing the Rite to Life," the purpose of which is to suggest some possible ways to let the sacraments continue to sustain us in ever new ways as we journey along in our faith life. These sections can aid us in seeing how relevant the sacraments are and also how they continue to grow and grace our lives. The sacraments, like our faith, are open ended, and this section can help us experience this reality.

To develop an ongoing awareness of the *sustaining* power of the sacraments, we must *bring the rite to life* by giving the sacraments a real and ongoing place in how we live our life. Just as we learn the things that better sustain our physical and mental well-being and avoid those things that would be detrimental, so we must also become aware of what to do or not to do in regard to the well-being of our spirit. All the sacraments begin in time. But all the sacraments point and lead to an eternal purpose and goal.

∞Sacrament of Baptism∞

Let us make humankind in our own image, according to our likeness... (Genesis 1:26).

The mission—called and sent

After his resurrection Christ gives this mission to his apostles: "Go therefore and make disciples of all nations, baptizing them in the name of the Father and of the Son and of the Holy Spirit, teaching them to observe all that I have commanded you. And remember, I am with you always, until the end of the age."[32]

This mission Jesus entrusts to the disciples is not a mission of conquering the world, but a mission of conversion; it is not a plan for attack, but a plan of invitation, recognition, and inclusion. During the time the disciples were with Jesus, listening to his words, watching his behavior, and slowly embracing him as *the Christ, the Anointed One,* the disciples experienced an inner conversion to see the world, others, and themselves in an ever-deepening and open relationship with God and themselves. This was a gradual process, and there were those moments when things got a little iffy.

Luke 9:51–55 tells us that Jesus was going to Jerusalem and wanted to stop at a Samaritan town along the way. So he sent messengers ahead to get things ready. But the Samaritans would not let Jesus and the disciples into their village because they were headed for Jerusalem. James and John were more than a bit put out by this and suggested to Jesus that he let them call down fire from heaven to consume the village. Jesus was not happy with their scorched-earth method of conquer and conversion. But we can't really blame them for resorting to that method of control. They probably learned that from being conquered and ruled by the Romans. So Jesus rebuked them, but he did not condemn them. Jesus knew that if they were going to follow him, they had to be born all over again in so many ways.

"Born again"

Being *born again*—or perhaps, *recognizing the life into which we have been born*—is central to understanding the teaching of Jesus. We know that it takes time for us to come to an understanding of life in the physical world into which we are born. In spending that time and energy to get to know our world, we can only go so deep. And yet our spirit yearns for more, which is the reason God gradually reveals and invites us to look deeper into ourselves and learn how God views our world…and so recognize the "fullness of life" into which we have been born. That revelation and invitation comes through Jesus, the Promised and Anointed One of God—the very "Word of God" as John tells us.

So often in our salvation history, the covenants God made—simple and straightforward in their making—became encrusted with rules and regulations and teachings that virtually hid the God who tried to reach out and embrace the people. "The God of Abraham, the God of Isaac, and the God of Jacob" became unrecognizable after a while. Moses had to ask God for a name so he could tell the people in Egypt who it was who was sending him. Time and again God sent prophets. For a while they were heard, and then some were killed and others were ignored. It seemed that God was unable to break through the small-mindedness and short-term memory of the people and their religious institutions.

But God did not give up on the children of the earth. At a certain time in history, a young Jewish maiden who was willing to simply trust that God would fulfill that age-old promise was also willing to become an agent, an active part, in fulfilling that promise according to God's will. Despite her fear and lack of understanding, she was willing to be overshadowed by the Spirit of God, and in her the Incarnate Word took on flesh and was born into our human condition. And everything Jesus, the Incarnate One, did and said was to help us understand that he was born into our humanity so that we could be born into his divinity through a *rebirth*. In fact without openness to the rebirth brought about again by the Spirit, we would not be able to fully understand and experience the Kingdom of God.

Rebirth—Nicodemus and the woman at the well

As we read in the Gospel of John, chapter 3, something about Jesus's teaching and ministry ignited a spark of interest in a person called Nicodemus. He was a Pharisee who heard about Jesus and the signs he performed. He came to Jesus by night. Nicodemus affirmed his belief that Jesus is "a teacher who has come from God." His belief was based on the signs Jesus performed. But Jesus wanted Nicodemus to see beyond the external signs. So Jesus invited him to *look again* and *be reborn* in his life and so "...enter the Kingdom of God." This *rebirth* happens in the *birth waters* of the Spirit. Nicodemus was already born of the flesh; now he was able to be born of the Spirit.

So how does this *rebirth*, this *born again of the Spirit,* play out in our lives? Our physical lives, as mysterious as they might be, are something of a given. We take them for granted. We just have them. They are celebrated each year with family and friends. They grow in us, and we grow in them. Hopefully, at some point in this growth, we begin to reflect on them, value them, take care of them, and come to some understanding of what it means to live. *Life* as we know it in our individual selves is more than just our physical selves. There is a *nonphysical* part of us that in some mysterious way is us as well. Little by little we become more and more aware of this life and what it offers us. By making choices the doors and windows of our life are opened, and some are closed. Some of the paths we choose are dead ends; others lead to places that are exciting and open. Our life is a journey into planned, as well as unforeseen, places. And when our physical bodies can no longer support this life in us, even as we linger at the end of it, there is some spark, some dynamic, in us that wants to go on and that urges us to hope for something more.

We see a great example of this played out in the Gospel account of John (4:1–42) when Jesus meets the Samaritan woman at the well. In the story of Nicodemus, it is night when Jesus speaks of the waters of birth as one begins *a life in the Spirit*. Jesus encounters the Samaritan woman at Jacob's well, and it is midday. There is no indication that the woman knew anything about Jesus. Seemingly, she had every intention of drawing water, filling her water jar, and returning home. Eventually that would happen, but she would return home with the revelation of *life-giving water,* the source of which she would find deep in her heart.

So the encounter begins with Jesus acknowledging that he is thirsty and asking the woman for a drink. After some initial sparring about race, gender, and what's required to draw water from the well, Jesus invites the woman to recognize first her *physical thirst* and then to the deeper *spiritual thirst* that she has tried to quench in so many unsuccessful ways. In doing so, Jesus quenches his own thirst and gives her the opportunity to allow him to quench her thirst for *that something or someone* that is the cause of her *thirst*.

To understand this *something more,* we must be born again, *be born from above,* or recognize that *spirit life* that is also *us.* "Born of water and the Spirit," Jesus says. Like Nicodemus we wonder, "How can these things be?" To this question, Jesus gives us the famous quote that we see so often simply as John 3:16: "For God so loved the world that he gave his only Son, so that everyone who believes in him may not perish but may have eternal life." Verse 17 continues, "Indeed, God did not send the Son into the world to condemn the world, but in order that the world might be saved through him."

Rebirth and salvation

And how was the world saved through him? It was not *"salvation by **condemning** the world"* but *"salvation by* *embracing the world,"* with the embrace of a God who so loved the world. And it is into this reality that Jesus invited the disciples to follow him, taught them, and then sent them on mission to invite the world to not only accept this *saving embrace* but to also extend this *saving embrace* to the corners of creation.

This *being born again* we make into a ritual in the action of baptizing. The act of baptizing is simple: immersion, pouring, or sprinkling with water. The act is accompanied with the simple but profound statement, using the words of Jesus, "I baptize you in the name of the Father and of the Son and of the Holy Spirit."

Like the human family embracing, welcoming, recognizing, and accepting the newborn as its own—and in doing so committing itself to the care and the well-being of the child—baptism is the act of the people of God embracing, welcoming, recognizing, and accepting this *newborn* (whatever the age of the person) as a *child of God*. It commits to the care and well-being of this *child of God*. This *child of God* is unique both in birth and in baptism, and thus the relationships that begin in being born and being *born again* are unique.

We are born into and need a human family to help us reach some degree of health and independence. We need to be nourished and cared for in many ways. We need to learn and understand how to survive and thrive in the world. We need to learn the wisdom of getting beyond our self-directedness to communicate and relate to other people in our life. We need to learn how to nourish and care for others as we have been given nourishment and care.

When we are *reborn*, we also need others to help us grow in spirit and in the Spirit. That Spirit family is called *Trinity—Father, Son, and Holy Spirit*—in whose name we have been baptized. In addition we become part of a faith family or family of faith. For some people, the designations *denomination* and *church* have negative connotations associated with them because of past experiences or because of their structure. I am using the terms *faith family* and *family of faith*, not because these terms are free from bad experiences (some of the most difficult and bad experiences happen in family) and not because they lack structure (families certainly have structure). The word *family* depicts the fundamental and natural social group into which we are born and through which we grow and mature. The *faith family* that recognizes and welcomes us as a child of God through *baptism, rebirth,* or being *born again* is special and unique because it is the gateway through which we become more aware of this journey of life in the Spirit.

The purpose of our human family is to help us grow to a point of freedom so that we can turn and freely and intentionally accept our place in the family. This is in order that what started as a physical and biological relationship of need can grow into family relationships based on freely chosen friendship and love. In the structure of family, our parents will always be *parent*, and we will always be *child*, but the bonds that hold us close are freely and uniquely chosen, and that makes all the difference. This prepares us for relating to the wider world.

And so it is with the family of faith (denomination, church, faith communities). The purpose of our faith family is to help us grow in Spirit and in grace to a point of freedom where we can turn and freely and intentionally accept our place as a member in this family of faith. And what started as perhaps a moment of emotion, enlightenment, or even fear can grow into relationships between members of the faith family that are based on friendship and love, in and through the community of Father, Son, and Holy Spirit. In our faith family, the structure will remain, but the bonds that hold us close are freely and uniquely chosen, and that too makes all the difference.

Each year, on a given date, a person can choose to celebrate his or her birth and the life that has been lived since that moment. It is usually celebrated with family and friends who have come to appreciate the uniqueness of who that person is and has become. Hopefully, the person has come to a realization that what he or she has become has been accomplished not only through his or her own efforts, but also through the care and concern of so many others—some known and many unknown. It is this recognition—"it takes a village to raise a child"—that opens an individual to the interconnectedness of the human family. Without this reflection or recognition, people can tend to think that they are self-made individuals, which, of course, is not true but rather an unfortunate and tragic lie. The love of self will never be sufficient enough to sustain a person's life for long or bring joy and happiness. There has to be a better and more certain way.

Sustaining rebirth and life

The good news is that there is! And the real good news (Gospel) is that there always has been a better and more certain way. The revelation revealed in the person of Jesus, namely God Incarnate, is to help us see that what happened in the Garden of Eden can be redeemed. After Adam and Eve willfully disobeyed, their eyes were opened to how naked, frail, and vulnerable they were without God. The original sin—which we inherit like a genetic pathology—can be forgiven and wiped away; the lie of the evil one can be exposed in the truth of the Anointed One. And the truth is that we can *again walk with the Lord God in the garden at the time of the evening breeze*. To do this, we have to recognize our true place in the family of God and return to our original nakedness by shedding all the ways we have tried to cover up what we thought was a weakness— namely, our being created and our dependency on God. The truth is that we come to realize that we are sustained in life because of our being created in love and by love. The purpose of this truth is to lead us into *original innocence*. This does not deny our sinful tendencies. Rather, it affirms the loving plan of God revealed in and by Jesus. This affirmation leads to confidence of spirit, which is sorely needed in a world focused primarily on itself and material things that do not satisfy.

There is the story of two brothers. One was very confident and optimistic, and the other had very poor self-esteem. In an attempt to build the confidence of the brother with poor self-esteem, the parents gave him a gold watch for Christmas. As soon as he opened the gift and saw what it was, he became very sad and said that he was afraid he would lose it or damage it. He was afraid to even put it on his wrist. There seemed to be no way the parents could help him overcome his lack of self-esteem.

The parents then told the child who was very self-confident and optimistic that his gift was in the backyard. When he ran outside and found a burlap sack with a red ribbon tied around it and filled with horse manure, he ran all around the yard looking for the pony he thought his parents had gotten for him.

Lack of self-esteem has emerged as a problem of epidemic proportion in our society. Millions of people are handicapped by damaged egos as they struggle to meet the challenges of everyday life. They are prevented from taking advantage of opportunities for enhanced living because they lack a basic sense of self-worth. Psychologists point out that lack of self-esteem has its roots in not feeling unconditionally lovable.

Defining words and blessing of baptism

No words in Scripture are more empowering than those words spoken by God to Jesus as Jesus presents himself to the prophet John for baptism: "This is my beloved Son. My favor rests on him." Another translation reads "You are my beloved; it gives me great pleasure to look upon you." (Compare Matthew 3:17, Mark 1:11, and Luke 3:22.)

Love transforms. Absolute love transforms absolutely. Jesus's clear recognition that he was loved so utterly by God energized his life and empowered him to begin his public ministry.

We would love to hear those words addressed to ourselves. Who would not want to know that God looks fondly upon us, that God is aware of our existence and cares about us? Who would not be moved in knowing that we give God great pleasure in our very being and that God loves us for who and what we are? We all want desperately to hear that we are unconditionally lovable, that we are ultimately worthwhile and valuable to someone significant. Such an affirmation is beyond all affirmations. It would radically change the way we look at ourselves and would increase our self-esteem beyond all bounds.

Well, the good news of the Gospel is precisely that these words were spoken not just to Jesus but, indeed, to each of us. And we must hear them and speak them in the midst of our faith community. That is precisely why the church has emphasized the Sacrament of Baptism as a Sacrament of Initiation. Its focus is communal and individual. Baptism is the sign that the community of our Creator, Redeemer, and Sanctifier commits itself to us, that we may be a bonded people of faith and worship and of unity and justice. Parents and the community of the faithful commit themselves to the baptized. They will walk together, faith-filled, with the baptized, each weekend of worship, each day of doing justice, fostering peace, and caring for others.

God does not pick and choose: "I will love this one; I will not love that one." Neither should we! God is absolute love and can only love absolutely, without restriction. God looks upon us and finds each of us utterly lovable. And this is the fundamental root of all genuine self-esteem. The Spirit of God's love comes upon each of us, and as we are infused with love, we in turn are to pour out the spirit of our love on each other.

Being baptized immerses us and rebirths us into the person of Jesus and the Kingdom of God. It reincarnates us by the working of the Spirit into what St. Paul called *the Body of Christ* and what Vatican Council II called *the People of God*.

Our human baptismal family

Our day of baptism is a day for new and renewed life in the Spirit. Some people celebrate that day. Most probably do not remember the date of their baptism. But each Easter we are given the opportunity to renew our baptismal promises followed by a blessing with the Easter baptismal waters. We celebrate with our faith family and friends who have come to appreciate both the uniqueness of each of us and what we have become. Hopefully, we come to a realization that what we have become has been accomplished not only through our own efforts, but also through the care and concern of so many others—some known and many unknown. It is this recognition (that it takes a community of faith to raise a child of God) that opens an individual to the interconnectedness of the faith family. Without this reflection or recognition, people can tend to think that they are self-made individuals, which, of course, is not reality. It is a repeat of the tragic lie spoken by the evil one in the Garden of Eden and the gardens of our hearts. Baptism does not take away our human tendencies or our freedom to choose. But being part of a faith community helps us to identify and be alert for such tendencies in ourselves and deal with them as the child of God that we are.

The human family into which we are born has a history, and although we share a common humanity, this history is replete with many divisions: race, tribe, culture, gender, and economic status, to name a few. These have their positive and negative effects on us. During our early years, we simply learn to live—as a member of a race, enculturated, female or male, poor, middle class, rich—with little or no awareness of the predisposed or prejudiced life we are living. In many ways we become the personification of these predispositions or prejudices. Maturing in our humanity, we will, hopefully, recognize our commonality and not permit our prejudices to continue or create artificial divisions. Maturing in our humanity, we will, hopefully, learn how to bridge these differences and divisions so that together we can live a life that is civilized and in harmony.

The family of faith into which we are *born* also has a history. Although we share a common bond of faith, our history of salvation is replete with divisions in what, how, and why we believe. Again, as we mature in faith, we, hopefully, will recognize our common belief and bond with God in and through Jesus. It is in and through Jesus, Incarnate and Redeemer, that we come to understand the sanctifying spirit of God the Creator, in whose name we have been baptized so that we can live our life in harmony with all people—which was Jesus's prayer at the Last Supper.

> *I ask not only on behalf of these [those present at the Last Supper], but also on behalf of those who will believe in me through their word, that they may all be one. As you, Father, are in me and I*

am in you, may they also be in us, so that the world may believe that you have sent me. The glory that you have given me I have given them, so that they may be one, as we are one, I in them and you in me, that they may become completely one, so that the world may know that you have sent me and have loved them even as you have loved me. (John 17:20–23).[33]

The teaching and prayer of Jesus always move in a positive, open, and Spirit-filled direction. We in the human family tend more toward the negative, closed, and self-filled direction. Father Richard Rohr points out in his book *Immortal Diamond, The Search For Our True Self,* "We have spent centuries of philosophy trying to understand the *problem of evil,* yet I believe the more confounding and challenging issue is the *problem of good.*"[34]

Even our religious institutions have been drawn into focusing more on *the problem of evil* than embracing *the problem of good.* But we have not been called to proclaim the *evil news.* We have been called to proclaim the *good news.* At the end of the Eucharistic Liturgy, we are dismissed with the words, "Go and announce the Good News of the Lord."

In baptism the focus is typically more about eliminating original sin than embracing original innocence. The focus is more about being made or becoming a child of God, rather than coming to recognize that we are children of God. That is not a subtle difference or just linguistic jargon. It is the same difference as *playing to win* and *playing not to lose.* In football it is called *prevent defense,* and it has never won a game. But coaches still use it and quite often lose because of it. The problem in *playing not to lose* is the change in attitude and mental positioning it takes. It is an attempt to play it safe. Actually, it changes the rhythm of the game; it is what actually puts a team into a winning position until they start *playing not to lose*. Changing that rhythm puts the team at risk.

The same is true when people focus only on their weakness and sinfulness and work *to make it to purgatory*, rather than embrace the truth of baptism—namely that it is about our original innocence and the child of God that we are. It goes to the very heart of the mystery of the Incarnation, and it clouds the fact that "God the Father of our Lord Jesus Christ has freed you from sin, given you a new birth by water and the Holy Spirit, and welcomed you into his holy people. He now anoints you with the chrism of salvation."[35] Baptism is the recognition and acceptance of that reality—first by the faith community and then by the one it embraces in baptism.

That is why we need a vibrant and dynamic faith community into which we are reborn. Again to quote Father Rohr, "We have to be taught how to look for anything infinite, positive, or good, which for some reason is much more difficult."[i] The power of the sacrament is meant to free us and empower us to bond ever more closely with the God who made us so that we can view the world with the mind of Jesus.

It must be noted that there are people of other religions who would not relate to God in the same way as Catholics or Christians might. Some people may not believe in God at all. But in their different belief, or choosing not to believe, they clearly have developed criteria for believing which is empowered or not by those around them. If the community of believers (or nonbelievers) does not accept and live this empowerment, the newly baptized (or initiated) will be at a distinct disadvantage.

Baptism is meant to direct our attention to the God-created image of the one baptized, yes. But it is also meant to direct the community's attention to the God-created image of all God's people. This helps to prepare us to love them enough to witness to the good news and recognize that although we may have earthly differences, we do not have Kingdom differences. "There is no distinction between Jew and Greek, slave and free, male and female" (Galatians 3:28). Our human DNA may separate us as distinct and unique, but our divine DNA unites and identifies us as one in the mystical and risen Body of Christ.

We receive the Sacrament of Baptism only once, but the grace of the sacrament is meant to enliven our every moment, our every thought, word, and deed. The grace of the sacrament tries to keep us rooted in the divine life as it empowers us to incarnate this very life of Christ by all we say and do. For this to happen, we must be open to the movement of God's Spirit in our lives. For this to happen, we must firmly believe that God loves us enough and trusts us enough to enliven our lives with the life-giving Spirit. To believe anything less is to misunderstand the promise of Jesus *to be with us always*, the ministry of Jesus *to meet people where they are,* and the invitation of Jesus *to come, follow me.*

Our birth and rebirth are open ended. We can live our human life limited by the thought of death, or we can live our human life with the knowledge that we have been given a share in the divine life that is coming to fulfillment, and death is but a moment of transition into the fullness of life. That was the promise Jesus gave Nicodemus and the woman at the well. And it is into this promise that we are baptized and reborn. It is something to celebrate every day of our lives, now and forever.

± Bringing the Rite to Life ±

*The greatest gift parents can give their children is
to love each other.*

The greatest gift children can give their parents is
to love each other.
The greatest gift God's children can give God...is to
love each other.

The cross—our sign of faith

For Catholics, almost every religious activity begins with this prayer: "In the name of the Father, and of the Son, and of the Holy Spirit. Amen." It has the effect of getting people's attention and letting everyone know that something is beginning. It's something of a greeting or signal. The depth of understanding can be varied.

We do a similar thing when we greet folks with "good morning." Those are the words, but they can be spoken in a variety of ways. They can be spoken in a casual way as we meet folks in the hall, and everyone continues on his or her way. Including a person's name and an added comment—like "how are you?" or "you look chipper!"—can expand them. In these cases, we may stop and chat for a moment. These words can be spoken as folks drowsily work their way to the breakfast table with just enough energy and enthusiasm to get the two words out in recognizable form to whomever might be around.

Awareness and attention span are disciplined habits we can and must develop to come to a fuller appreciation of the things that we do and the words that we say and hear. Otherwise, we can easily be drowsily working our way through life mouthing sweet or not-so-sweet nothings and wondering why we aren't understood and appreciated. If we want authentic communication to take place, we must become aware of what we say and how we say it and why we say it.

The simple statement "in the name of the Father, and of the Son, and of the Holy Spirit" is packed with meaning in terms of relationship, union, and mission. It claims a relationship with the Trinity (the God family): Creator and Father, Redeemer and Son, Sanctifier and Spirit. It claims union with the very Trinity in whose name we act. It claims recognition of the mission given us by Christ. It is a statement that is usually accompanied by making the sign of the cross on our bodies or foreheads.

These are the first words and actions that welcome the one to be initiated and baptized. After the name of the child or adult is made known, the reason for being there (what do you ask of God's church?) is stated (baptism). "Do you understand what you are asking?" is then asked. That understanding is centered on learning and living the commandments by loving God and neighbor.

At this point the person to be baptized is welcomed into the faith community with these words: "The Christian community welcomes you with great joy. In its name I claim you for Christ our Savior by the sign of his cross." At which point, in the case of a child, the parents, godparents, and other family members are invited to do the same; in the case of adults, it is the sponsors who participate.

When working with parents preparing for the baptism of their child, I think it is an excellent opportunity to let them know that they can and should continue that simple ritual of signing the child with those words, "in the name of the Father, and of the Son, and of the Holy Spirit." Think of all the times a parent kisses the child, embraces the child, puts the child to sleep, and drops the child off with a caregiver. Blessing the child is part and parcel of the parent's ministering duty and privilege. It keeps and renews the baptismal moment for the parents. As the children get older and can understand, it can help children come to know that, as they have a personal relationship with their parents, they also have a personal relationship with their Creator God, in whose image and likeness they are.

As children get older and watch others being baptized in the churches, there is little with which they can connect. But if they see the action of blessing and signing as something that their parents continue to do, it would draw them into what is happening at the moment.

Obviously, to try and initiate such a practice with older children, especially teens, would depend on the sensitivity of the child or teen. High fives tend to replace hugs, and bumping knuckles replaces other signs of affection.

Remembering our baptism

We regularly celebrate our birthday each year, but the date of our baptism can get lost in time. Some families have a Bible that has a section for recording the dates and places where sacraments are received. If that is available, one can write the parish where one is baptized and get a baptism certificate. When other sacraments are received, that information is typically sent to the church of baptism. When a new certificate is issued, all that information is on the baptism certificate. Simply noting one's day of baptism on the calendar can be an annual reminder to pray for one's parents and godparents.

As we listen to the scriptures being proclaimed at various services, we might recall that at our baptism there was the Ephphatha (be opened) prayer said as our lips and ears are signed with the cross so that we might be open to speaking and hearing the Word of God.

When we see candles lighted—and especially the Easter or Paschal Candle—we might envision our baptismal candle being lighted by our godparents and handed to our parents (or directly to us if we were older) as they are reminded that the light of Christ is entrusted to them. Hopefully, we too can see the spark of that light still burning in our hearts.

In our churches and in many homes, the water of baptism—holy water—is available. So when we bless ourselves using the same prayer with which we were baptized, we can be reminded of the reality that we are still growing and maturing into our baptismal identity as a beloved child of God. We continue to be nourished by a faith community of which we are a nourishing member.

Each time we profess our faith at Mass, we are renewing the promises made for us or that we ourselves made at our baptism. Now we do so with the words of the Nicene Creed. During the Easter season, we use the same words as we renew our promises.

At our baptism we are given the prayer that Jesus taught us. We are invited at every Eucharistic liturgy to echo that prayer through the years of our life. Like a child who stumbles over the words "I lub you" that grow ever more clearly through the years into "I love you," with a depth that knows no limit, so our praying the "Our Father" grows from a form we memorized into an enriched statement and recognition of our relationship with the God who feeds us daily and who invites us to feed others with mercy rendered.

It is good to reread the prayers of the rite of baptism periodically. So often we concentrate on the doing of the rite so we can get it correct, and that is normal. But in some quiet moments, just allowing the richness of the prayers to seep in can bring a new and enduring meaning. The last part of the baptism includes three short prayers that speak to the multidimensional reality of baptism.

The first is the blessing of the mother:

God the Father, through his Son, the Virgin Mary's child, has brought joy to all Christian mothers, as they see the hope of eternal life shine on their children. May [God] bless the mother of this child. She now thanks God for the gift of her child. May she be one with [her child] in thanking [God] forever in heaven, in Christ Jesus our Lord. All: Amen.

The second is the blessing of the father:

God is the giver of all life, human and divine. May he bless the father of this child. He and his wife will be the first teachers of their child in the ways of faith. May they be also the best of teachers, bearing witness to the faith by what they say and do, in Christ Jesus our Lord. All: Amen.

(Obviously, using the name of the mother, father, and child makes it so much more personal.)

The third blessing is of the community:

By God's gift, through water and the Holy Spirit, we are reborn to everlasting life. In goodness, may [God] continue to pour out blessings upon these sons and daughters. May [God] make them always, wherever they may be, faithful members of [God's] holy people. May [God] send peace upon all who are gathered here, in Christ Jesus our Lord. All: Amen.

Finally, when we attend the funeral of loved ones or members of our community of faith, we see some of the symbols that were used at baptism. The body or cremains are received by the name of the deceased and blessed with holy water and then clothed with a white pall. This person—this child of God—is called by the name, blessed with water recalling his or her baptism, and clothed again with the white garment and is received again by the community of faith. The deceased is then recognized as a person who has heard the Word of God and has held close the cross of Christ. The community that welcomed him or her into its midst now accompanies the person on the last earthly journey with baptism symbols that will birth them into eternal life.

The rite of the Sacrament of Baptism has a place and time. Let us pray that the fruit of the sacrament becomes an integral part of our life now and forever.

∞The Sacrament of Confirmation∞

Be *the change you wish to see in the world.*—Mohandas Gandhi

Enriched by the Spirit—empowered to witness

The document of the Second Vatican Council, *Lumen Gentium,* states that "by the sacrament of Confirmation, [the baptized] are more perfectly bound to the Church and are enriched with a special strength of the Holy Spirit. Hence they are, as true witnesses of Christ, more strictly obliged to spread and defend the faith by word and deed" (*Lumen Gentium* 11).[37]

The two basic statements, that "the baptized are more perfectly bound to the Church" and that they "are enriched with a special strength of the Holy Spirit" are all about *becoming aware* of what takes place at baptism and embracing that awareness to the extent that we understand it. The word "confirmation" means *ratifying, establishing, corroboration, and verification*—just to name a few of its designations. So one way we can look at the sacrament is that at our confirmation we acknowledge the bond of faith we have with the faith community (to the extent that we understand it at that moment), and through the laying on of hands and the anointing with chrism by the bishop or priest, members of the faith community accept and ratify our decision as they invoke and celebrate the strength of the Holy Spirit at work in us.

There still remains debate and confusion as to if and when there is a best time for the bestowing and celebrating of the Sacrament of Confirmation. At one time, confirmation was celebrated at the time of baptism as an integral part of the baptismal rite itself. Those baptized were adults who were baptized by elders or presbyters—deacons for the men and deaconesses for the women—and then led together into the midst of the assembly to be confirmed by the chief elder or bishop who represented the whole Christian community. With the dispersion of the Christian community, its growth in numbers, infant baptism, and other variables, the laying on of hands and anointing with chrism were delayed until the visit of the bishop and thus became separated from the rite of baptism.

The question then becomes whether or not the Sacrament of Baptism is incomplete until the laying on of hands and the anointing with chrism of the Sacrament of Confirmation. As far as the sacraments are concerned, this is a question for liturgists and theologians. But we know, in our family life, that at some point and in some way—conscious or not—even though we are children of our parents and related to siblings and others by blood, we must mature to a point when we intentionally accept them as such and celebrate who we are as a unique human family. Not to do so would weaken any relationships that might be there. And we know that failing to do so has its own negative consequences.

The lived dynamics in the human family are things into which we grow more or less day-to-day and little-by-little. There are many ways to celebrate our family, and most families do celebrate who they are as family to some degree—especially at birthdays, weddings, reunions, and gatherings when a family member dies. There is also a point at which each member of the family becomes more responsible for the family as a whole. Again these moments are experienced in different ways given the age and circumstances of the people involved. Parents instill and teach this responsibility in various fashions: children are taught to put their toys away, chores are assigned, newspapers are delivered, errands are run, and thank-you notes are written, just to name a few. All of these ways of becoming aware and bonding as a family can be seen in the spirit exhibited by the family. This *family spirit* is larger than any individual member. It evolves from the members of the family becoming a distinct entity of love binding all the members into one.

We know that there is a time in family life when the children grow into independence. This time can be a smooth transition or one filled with conflict—conflict within the individual person or between family members because of choices that are made or not made. These points of tension can be destructive to family ties, or they can be opportunities for a much stronger family bond—a way to confirm the family bond or to put off, and perhaps even deny, the family bond.

To strengthen that basic and fundamental bond of being family, we do things and make events that celebrate our being a family. In doing so, parents teach their children, and are taught themselves, how important it is to continue choosing and confirming each other as family. In an age of rugged and self-directed individualism and *all-about-me* privacy (which militates against both who we are as a family and who we are as a nation), families must create these moments or the basic bond that holds society together will erode, and then everyone will suffer. We will evolve into a kingdom of fantasy where each person bestows titles and entitlements on himself or herself. Lest this happen, we must confirm and be confirmed as responsible members of a family; then and only then will our human family begin to realize its potential.

The same is true for us in our faith family. The Sacrament of Confirmation is a sacred event by which a person reaffirms his or her baptism and membership within a faith community and accepts responsibility for the spread of the Gospel through the power of the Holy Spirit to the degree he or she is able. Like baptism the Sacrament of Confirmation itself stands alone as an event at a particular time when certain requirements are fulfilled. However, the preparation for the sacrament and the realization and awareness of the effects of the sacrament are the work of a lifetime, to the extent that we commit to the movement of the Spirit in us. Even though we receive the sacraments of baptism and confirmation only once liturgically or ritually, our rebirthing and being anointed with the Spirit is an ongoing, everyday experience. Sometimes we are even aware of it. Most of the time, however, we are not, until such time as we have learned to intentionally pay attention.

To get to that point, we must understand that our spirit life (which includes every aspect of our life) and life in the Spirit (which informs every aspect of our life) are a series of still pictures that are always moving. But even as we try to focus on a particular still picture—and that is usually something from the past—our life continues to move. To focus and come to an understanding of the moving *now,* we must give ourselves over to the movement of the Spirit confirmed in our life. The work of the Spirit is to help us reflect on our experience and live our life within the reality of the *now moments.* That is the only place we can engage and use our natural gifts as well as the gifts the Spirit gives us.

The Spirit always comes with gifts

This is not to discard the past or ignore the future. But we can only engage the *past* and the *future* in the *now*. And the Spirit strengthens us with gifts so that we can engage those *now moments* with *graced* results. That is exactly what the community of faith, through the bishop, prays for and acknowledges at the time of confirmation.

> *All-powerful God, Father of our Lord Jesus Christ, by water and the Holy Spirit you freed your sons and daughters from sin and gave them new life. Send your Holy Spirit upon them to be their helper and guide. Give them the spirit of wisdom and understanding, the spirit of right judgment and courage, the spirit of knowledge and reverence. Fill them with the spirit of wonder and awe in your presence. We ask this through Christ our Lord.[38]*

In the Sacrament of Baptism, the faith community acknowledges a person as a child of God. In the Sacrament of Confirmation, the faith community acknowledges the ongoing work of the Holy Spirit in the life of this child of God. That work of the Spirit is to enrich this child of God with the ability to bring wisdom, understanding, right judgment, courage, knowledge, reverence, wonder, and awe to the family of faith in particular, and to the world in general, in each and every *now moment*. Those gifts do not work in the past or the future—only now. And there is a reason: the Spirit is helping us come to an understanding of the *eternal now*. These gifts of Spirit enable us to imitate, witness, and do the work of God as Jesus did. It is the same Spirit at work in us that was at work in him.

This is made evident in the Gospel of John. It is the Paschal Meal (the Last Supper). Jesus has washed the feet of the disciples, even over Peter's objections. Jesus then foretells his betrayal by one of them. Obviously, they want to know who it is and, obviously, it is one of them. To help them deal with whatever happens, Jesus gives them the new commandment of love. "Just as I have loved you, you also should love one another" (John 13:34). Right on cue, Peter steps up and declares his willingness to follow Jesus even if it means laying down his life for him. Jesus then foretells his denial. By this time the disciples have to be very confused. What is happening? What started out as a celebration and commemorative meal has turned into chaos. What is going on?

In the midst of this confusion, Jesus says, "Do not let your hearts be troubled." Then he proceeds to tell them that there are many dwelling places in the house of the Father. Actually, he is going to prepare a place for them so that they may be where he is going. Then he tells them that they know the way.

Peter is not the only one who speaks up. It seems that the disciples have gained their voice. So Thomas takes his turn: "Lord, we do not know where you are going. How can we know the way?" That is a very important question, and it needed to be asked—not just for the sake of the apostles, but for our sake as well.

So Jesus said to him and to us, "I am the way, and the truth, and the life. No one comes to the Father except through me. If you know me, you will know my Father also. From now on you do know him and have seen him."

Then Philip, probably reflecting the mind of many of the others, says, "Lord, show us the Father, and we will be satisfied." Jesus is probably very excited that these questions are taking form in the minds of the disciples. He had given them the answers, just like *Jeopardy*, and they are coming up with the correct questions.

So Jesus said to him, "Whoever has seen me has seen the Father. Do you not believe that I am in the Father and the Father is in me? The words that I say to you I do not speak on my own; but the Father who dwells in me does his works. Believe me that I am in the Father and the Father is in me; but if you do not, then believe me because of the works themselves."

But then Jesus lets them know that the work of proclamation doesn't stop with him. Up till this moment, he has told them who he is and why he has come. Now, to add to their wonderment, he tells them that he is leaving and why he is leaving: "Very truly, I tell you, the one who believes in me will also do the works that I do and, in fact, *will do greater works than these*, because I am going to the Father."

Then Jesus speaks to them of the gift of the Spirit that is theirs as well and how they will grow into being empowered. Jesus will not leave them orphaned but will be always available to them. The Father will give them another Advocate that will abide with them forever.

In those twenty verses of John (14:1–20) we have a *MapQuest* plan to follow: Jesus, the Christ and Redeemer, is the way to God, the Creator and Father; and the Holy Spirit, the Advocate and Sanctifier, is the way to Jesus. The work of the Holy Spirit is to help us to recognize not just the Jesus of history but also the very Christ image in ourselves and in each other. This coming to know our *true self* is not a *messiah complex* but the recognition that we have been anointed, and in this anointing we have been called to do the works of the Anointed One and *even greater works than these,* Jesus says. Where do we get the strength for this?

The Spirit's gift of community

In a Peanuts cartoon, Linus is watching television. Into the family room storms Lucy. Putting her fist right into his face, Lucy demands that Linus change the channel to the one she wants to watch. "What makes you think you can just walk right in here and take over?" Linus wants to know.

"These five fingers! Individually they are nothing. But when I curl them into a single unit, they form a weapon that is terrible to behold!"

Linus shrinks back and says, "Ah, ha, so what channel did you want to watch?" As Lucy takes what was his place in front of the TV, Linus looks at his own fingers. "Why can't you guys get organized like that?"

I suspect that Jesus thinks the same thing when he looks at his disciples and at us: "Why can't you guys get organized like that?" Jesus begins his ministry by calling simple fishermen to join him. Later tax collectors, farmers, laborers, and peasants will join his band—all hardworking but ordinary, undistinguished individuals, whose faith brings them together as a church that is capable of doing great things.

I suspect they all had their reasons for answering that call, and as the story of their call unfolds, we know that they were a mixed bag. The promise of a Messiah who would bring about a kingdom of peace and justice for the ordinary folk was a powerful belief. People were looking for a new millennium. They wanted to get rid of oppression and live their lives freely. So there was little thought as to the cost of discipleship.

We, too, want to live our lives free of oppression. The president's State of the Union address every year is filled with hopes of that happening. There is much talk about benefits, little said about cost. There is much said about surplus, little said about the debt. Keeping the myth of how well off we are, without working to make it real, seems to be the predominant political spin.

Gambling is one of the fastest growing addictions in the United States today, revealing that there is a tendency to want to get something for nothing—or at least with a minimum amount of effort. Investors want big payoffs with the least amount of risk. Millions of people want all kinds of benefits, but are they willing to pay the price?

How often we hear that in life there are no free lunches— at least not over a long period of time. If we want a good education, we work hard for it. If we want our marriages and family life to prosper, it will take a lot of good will and effort. This is a lesson confirmed in the scriptures. Zebulun and Naphtali, two lost tribes of Israel who were first to fall to the invading Assyrians, receive a promise: "Those that walked in darkness, they will see a great light" (Isaiah 8:23). This is the area where Jesus grew up. But some people chose to remain in the dark because the Kingdom of Light has its price. Light shows all. And so to prepare ourselves, Jesus tells us simply, "Repent!"

All of us would relish a life of peace, love, kindness, and compassion. We wish harmony existed among all people and that trust and tolerance were universally in evidence. We speak passionately about ideals but often fall short of the practical discipline required to make them real. We want the benefits of kingdom living, but we do not want the change in vision and lifestyle that makes these benefits possible.

But are we willing to repent and make the teachings of Jesus a practical part of everyday life? Are we willing to apply our Christian principles to our daily actions? When will we stop edging God out of our lives by protesting that the world is too complex today to mix faith and politics, faith and financial decisions, faith and sports, or faith and personal relationships? What is most evident to those with the courage to look is that when we relegate God and faith to the sidelines, life as we know it diminishes and collapses into a meaningless struggle.

A community at risk

When the Corinthians chose to argue about whose side they were on, the church at Corinth was in danger of collapsing. (See 1 Corinthians 1:10–17.) Throughout his ministry, Jesus had to consistently remind the disciples where they had to keep focus.

It is not just a hope that God's Kingdom may come. It is a willingness to share in the bringing about of that kingdom. St. Teresa of Avila has written a prayer that speaks powerfully to this reality.

Christ has no body but yours,
No hands, no feet on earth but yours,
Yours are the eyes with which he looks
Compassion on this world,
Yours are the feet with which he walks to do good,
Yours are the hands, with which he blesses all the world.
Yours are the hands, yours are the feet,
Yours are the eyes, you are his body.
Christ has no body now but yours,
Christ has no body now on earth but yours.[39]

No one can do it alone. But when we take faith-filled individuals and join them into a *single unit* of faith, *what a source of power* they can be!

The "overshadowing power" of the Spirit

From the very beginning of creation, the Spirit of God was at work. "In the beginning when God created the heavens and the earth, the earth was a formless void and darkness covered the face of the deep, while the Spirit of God swept over the face of the waters" (Genesis 1:1–2). This overshadowing— this sweeping over by the Spirit of God—brought order and form to chaos, light to darkness, life to nothingness, and humankind in the image of God (Genesis 1:27). This same Spirit of God will walk with humankind "in the garden at the time of the evening breeze" (Genesis 3:8). In spite of rejection by created humanity, gifted with free will, the Spirit of God will overshadow this rejection with a covenant and promise of redemption. This covenant and promise was made known in revelation to and by patriarchs and prophets inspired by this same Spirit through time.

When the Spirit of God overshadowed Mary at her *Fiat*, the fulfillment of God's promise to send the Messiah began in time. God descended into time in the womb of Mary—thus the Incarnation: God taking on our human condition in time. At Christmas we celebrate the birth of Jesus the Christ, the Anointed One, and God-made visible, signed with a human body.

This visibility of Emmanuel (God with us) begins, in time, the fulfillment of *the promise of redemption*, which the patriarchs and prophets consistently and often reveal. The Spirit of God overshadows John the Baptist as he proclaims Jesus, the Christ. Then the Spirit of God descends upon Jesus, confirming Jesus, the Anointed One and the one who pleases God and is God's beloved.[40]

The work of the Holy Spirit is very evident in the final days Jesus spends with the disciples. It begins with a triumphal entry into Jerusalem. (See John 12:12–15.) John then states,

"His disciples did not understand these things at first; but when Jesus was glorified, then, they remembered that these things were written of him and had been done to him" (John 12:16). The disciples were in their own comfort zone and were clueless about what happened and what was happening. It would only be at a later time, after the sorrowful and traumatic events of the next several days, weeks, and months, that they would allow the Spirit to disengage them from their fears, arrogance, and their shame that they held on to so stubbornly. The Spirit had to lead them to faith again in the midst of their refusal to believe the reality of the empty tomb and what that meant. The Spirit had to enlarge and expand what and how they believed about Jesus and themselves. They had all heard the invitation to "come, follow me" at their initial encounter with Jesus (John 1:35), and they would hear it again at their last encounter. (See John 21:19.)

The Spirit quietly nudged them gently sometimes and at other times got their attention with *a mighty wind and tongues of fire.* It seemed that the disciples, well intentioned as they were, had to learn the language and the movement of the Advocate that Jesus promised and sent. They no longer had the physical presence of Jesus sitting in their midst teaching and correcting them. Now they needed to learn how to know and understand the presence of the Spirit. If they were to "go therefore and make disciples of all nations..." (Matthew 28:19), they had to learn a fundamental trust in the Spirit.

We have already seen an example of that in Acts chapter 10, when Peter encountered Cornelius. When Jesus promised the disciples that he would not leave them orphans but would send an Advocate to guide them, he did not intend to put them on autopilot. And the history of Christianity has proven that it has been everything but autopilot. Each generation and each individual has to learn the language and the movement of this seemingly elusive Spirit of God. We must learn how to listen and to whom to listen.

Isaiah listened (as recorded in chapter 11, verse 2) and presents us with the gifts of the Spirit: *wisdom and understanding, counsel and might, knowledge and the fear of the Lord.*[41]

Openness to these Gifts will help us learn how to listen.

As to whom to listen to, Paul's letter to the Galatians gives us a way to test the work of the Spirit, namely by the fruit produced: *"love, joy, peace, patience, kindness, generosity, faithfulness, gentleness, and self-control…If we live by the Spirit, let us also be guided by the Spirit"* (Galatians 5:22, 25).[42]

In the Gospel of Luke, we have an example of this elusive Spirit at work as we are told the story about the two disciples on the road to Emmaus after the death of Jesus and how Jesus joined them on their way and how they did not recognize him until they recognized him in the breaking of the bread. (See Luke 24:13–35.) This *breaking of bread* is the expression the first Christians used to designate their Eucharistic assemblies. (Acts 2:42, 46; 20:7, 11)

Community united

This *breaking of bread* is an action of remembrance and recognition. In the *breaking of bread* the Spirit leads us to remember and make present the action of Jesus at the Last Supper and to recognize the presence of the Risen Christ in this action of giving and receiving the Bread of Life and the Chalice of Salvation. It is in participating in this action that we become a Eucharistic assembly led by the Spirit to remember and recognize the presence of the Risen Christ.

The Sacrament of Confirmation is an opportunity to acknowledge our baptism into Christ and is a sign that we are marked and strengthened for public ministry. And this brings us to both the source and summit of our strengthening, namely, the Sacrament of Eucharist—the body and blood of Christ.

± Bringing the Rite to Life ±

The Spirit leads

In the Gospel of Mark we read where Jesus is baptized, confirmed as the Beloved One of God, and led by the Spirit into the desert to be tempted.

> *At that time Jesus came from Nazareth in Galilee and was baptized by John in the Jordan. As Jesus was coming up out of the water, he saw heaven being torn open and the Spirit descending on him like a dove. And a voice came from heaven: "You are my Son, whom I love; with you I am well pleased." At once the Spirit sent him out into the desert, and he was in the desert forty days, being tempted by Satan. He was with the wild animals, and angels attended him.*[3]

The Sacrament of Confirmation focuses on this same Spirit as a gift given to us and invites us to embrace and follow this Spirit as Jesus did. Matthew tells us that Jesus was led by the Spirit to be tested in the desert. After a long period of fasting, Jesus is obviously hungry. Just as in Genesis, the tempter tries to catch Jesus at a moment of human need. The tempter suggests that he turn the stones into bread. Notice how subtle the temptation is, not unlike the temptation in Genesis. The tempter addressed the hunger *for the knowledge of good and evil,* promising something they already had: likeness to God, which obviously they had lost sight of. Jesus doesn't fall for this trickery. Jesus knows who he is; the Spirit had just confirmed that at the Jordan. Jesus also knows the source of life and what it is that nourishes his hunger.

The tempter then tested this faith of Jesus: "If you believe you are the Son of God...throw yourself down." We will hear something similar on Calvary. Jesus knows he is the Son of God, or as John says, the Word of God. He doesn't need to test it.

All subtlety disappears in the third temptation. The tempter offers Jesus *the world*—everything—"if you will fall down and worship me." And here is where Jesus gives us a powerful insight. When we "worship the Lord [our] God, and serve [God] alone," we will have enough.

The lessons we can take from Jesus's sojourn in the desert and his encounter with the tempter are as follows:
- Be firm in faith and beware the subtleties of temptations.
- Know we are children of God, and never let anyone move us to doubt that.
- The tempter promises everything and delivers nothing good or lasting. God alone suffices.

The gifts and tools for a life of faith

The same Spirit that sent Jesus into the desert, fortified with the gifts and tools to withstand the temptations posed by the good and the evil, is the same Spirit that sends us into our lives and the confrontations we experience with the good and the evil. To help us to come to know and distinguish good and evil, we are given the gifts of the Spirit.

Wisdom is the gift by which we come to value properly the things we are taught and believe through faith. Wisdom helps us to develop a proper relationship with the world around us.

Understanding is the gift that helps us gain, through experience and reflection, growing certitude about the values that faith leads us to embrace.

Counsel is the gift that helps us to maintain an openness to being led by the Spirit so that we can judge how best to behave and act in the circumstances of our lives.

Fortitude gives us the strength and balance to follow through faithfully in our thinking and behaving in the face of life's pressures and conflicts.

Knowledge is the gift that is birthed from our faith experiences and helps us to see the circumstances in life as God sees them, which aids us in determining meaning and purpose in our lives.

Piety is the gift that helps us recognize and honor the place that God, our Creator, should have in our daily lives. Piety is a way of thinking, seeing, and accepting God's loving Presence by loving that Presence in return.

Fear of the Lord is the gift that keeps us from offending. It is a gift that arises from our love of a God we simply do not want to offend. As we grow in our sense of the awesomeness of God, the mercy of God, and the unconditional love of God, our fear of offending such a God helps us avoid whatever might belittle our relationship with God.

In the temptation story, we can see that Jesus manifested the gifts the Spirit gave him as he dealt with each of the temptations. The first temptation was to raise a doubt in the mind of Jesus: "if you are the Son of God..." If the evil one can get us to doubt our relationship with God, then we open ourselves to a loss of balance and meaning. It happened to Adam and Eve in the garden when they were deceived. It didn't happen to Jesus, and it need not happen to us if we are on our guard for the lie. We are children of God, and we best not forget it, or we too will be deceived.

The second temptation was for Jesus to prove to himself that God loved him by jumping from the parapet of the temple. Jesus knew better. God doesn't make us jump through hoops to earn love. God simply unconditionally loves us and invites us to recognize that reality.

The third temptation was the promise of power over the earth—a promise that was not delivered in the case of Adam and Eve and a promise that evil can never deliver. Again Jesus was not about to deny who he was in his relationship to God nor was he going to ask God to prove God's love for him, and certainly he was not going to trade the reign of God for earthly power—nor should we.

But to do this, we have to accept and use the gifts of the Spirit that the Sacrament of Confirmation reveals that we have. These are gifts for maturing as God's children. They are practical and critical gifts we can use to live our earthly life in freedom. They help us to recognize the difference between truth and lies, between what is authentic and what is forgery, and between what is solid and what is just veneer.

Monitoring our growth in the Spirit

To help us to monitor how we are doing, we can look to what kind of fruit our efforts bear. Again the Holy Spirit offers us ways of seeing and evaluating our efforts, providing we are willing to accept such insight. If the things we spend our time and money on help to bring about in ourselves a spirit of love, joy, and peace; if the things we attempt are done with patience, kindness, and goodness; if we grow more comfortable with long-suffering, mildness, and faith; if our thoughts and behavior reflect moderation, modesty, and chastity; then we need not worry. Obviously none of this happens at once, and it takes effort and practice—like anything worth doing.

And there are practical ways to proclaim Gospel values in our life. Abraham Maslow has given us a theory in psychology that proposes that human beings must have their basic physical and emotional needs met before they can realize their fullest potential. We are able to help others satisfy those needs. Matthew, chapter 25, enumerates several ways we can do this: feed the hungry; give drink to the thirsty; clothe the naked; be concerned about the homeless; visit the sick. These can also be listed as corporal works of mercy. One can help or support a local food bank or kitchen that cares for people who are struggling. We can sort out of our closets clothes that are good but are not being worn, and we can give those clothes to thrift shops or homeless shelters. Besides friends and family who may be sick at home or in the hospital, there are people who are in assisted living or care centers who aren't sick but who have no one to visit them. They may be members of our parish or neighbors of ours who can no longer live alone. And when we make such visits, if appropriate, children should go along. It is a good way for children to gently know about people growing old and know that they are being cared for.

There are two other items on the list that might seem somewhat dated to us: ransom the captive, and bury the dead. We know from the news that in some areas of the world, people are captured and held for ransom. That seems so distant and beyond our ability to help. But I'm sure we all know people who are held captive by some addiction or another. Today sex trafficking in the United States and elsewhere, which had not been getting much attention is beginning to be addressed internationally. This kind of enslavement is particularly difficult to address. But ways and ministries to help victims, most often girls, are beginning to develop. Perhaps there are members of our family who are held captive by an addiction. Perhaps there are ways we can help them escape such enslavement. We can encourage them to get help. We certainly can put them on our prayer list.

We have professional funeral directors who bury the dead. But to bury the dead is not just placing a corpse in the ground. To bury the dead involves how we remember and respect the one who has died, how we support the family and friends of the one who has died, and how we do those things reflects our belief about death itself. Here again, when and where appropriate, children should be gently exposed to the reality of illness and death. It's a way of letting them see that people are still loved even when they are sick or have died. When we try to do all these things with a sincere heart, then we are proclaiming—with the help of the Spirit—the Gospel we say we believe.

Besides the corporal works of mercy, the Spirit empowers us to instruct the ignorant by helping people become aware of the fact that they are made in the image and likeness of God; to counsel the doubtful by encouraging them to have faith in God and confidence in the fact that God's love is unconditional; to proclaim to sinners that God forgives them and admonish them not to give in to shame and despair; to bear wrongs patiently and forgive those who wrong us; to comfort the afflicted by perhaps simply being present to them if that is all we can do; to pray for the living and the dead in a way that is intentional and caring. These spiritual works of mercy also help us to bear fruit in ways that confirm us as evangelists of the Gospel in company with the people of God. These are some of the ways that can help us bring the rite of confirmation to life as we grow as children of God anointed by the Spirit.

The rite of the Sacrament of Confirmation has a place and time. Let us pray that the fruit of the sacrament becomes an integral part of our life now and forever.

∞The Sacrament of Eucharist∞

From the moment you put a piece of bread in your mouth you are part of the world…Who made the bread? Where did it come from? You are in relationship to the guy (or gal) who made this stuff. And what is your relationship to him (or her)? Do you deserve to be eating this stuff…do you have a right to it? That is the world and that is no illusion.[43]

Thomas Merton

The reality of presence

The truth that Thomas Merton is alluding to is absolutely critical to our understanding the reality in which we live. It is the reality of relationship. There is not one moment in our existence in which we are not in relationship. There are the obvious ones, of course, and they are very real for us—our family, our circle of friends, and neighbors, for instance. Then there is our relationship to our history, culture, and environment. But Merton is suggesting that we be attentive to the less obvious relationships in our lives by reflecting upon the simple human act of eating bread. It is not about knowing the people by name that helped bring it to our table. But it is very much about being aware of our dependency on the people, whom we do not know, who helped bring it to our table. That realization of dependency is key to understanding *community, relationship, and presence.* And bread, along with wine, is the sign that Jesus chose to help us to remember.

Merton suggests that we use bread as a starting point to understand the reality of our dependence in the world. This is the only path to knowing our *true self*—that is, realizing our dependency on others. We need to embrace it and let it speak to us about our common unity. Each person who helped to bring bread to our table left something of his or her presence in that effort. That is why we should be grateful and give thanks because we have encountered the gift and power of presence in such a simple action as eating bread. It was in this action of eating bread at the Passover meal with his disciples that Jesus became the One Presence in the bread, broken, and the cup, shared. It is in remembrance of Jesus that we do this. It is the path to knowing our *true self*—that is, realizing our dependency on the divine. We need to embrace it and let it speak to us about our common union with the divine. We are grateful, and we give thanks because we have encountered the gift and power of presence in such a simple act as eating bread and drinking of the cup of salvation.

The real Spirit and presence

The scriptures reveal the Spirit of God overshadowing Jesus, the Anointed One, throughout his life on earth and throughout his ministry in the midst of the people. Jesus is the Word of God proclaimed and proclaiming—visible, accessible, and touchable—and divinely situated in time in our human condition. This incarnation—this being made visible, accessible, and touchable—did not end after Jesus's three-year public ministry, during which not only did people reach out to see and touch him, but also he intentionally reached out to see, touch, and nourish them.

This dynamic *being present* reached its summit during the Last Supper when Jesus said, "I have eagerly desired to eat this Passover with you before I suffer, for, I tell you, I will not eat it until it is fulfilled in the kingdom of God." Then he took a cup, and after giving thanks he said, "Take this and divide it among yourselves; for I tell you that from now on I will not drink of the fruit of the vine until the Kingdom of God comes." Then he took a loaf of bread, and when he had given thanks, he broke it and gave it to them, saying, "This is my body, which is given for you. Do this in remembrance of me." And he did the same with the cup after supper, saying, "This cup that is poured out for you is the new covenant in my blood."[44]

Matthew, Mark, and the quote from Luke cited above are very similar in their telling of the event. Paul tells us that what he received from the Lord, he passed on to the Corinthians: "That the Lord Jesus on the night when he was betrayed took a loaf of bread, and when he had given thanks, he broke it and said, 'This is my body that is for you. Do this in remembrance of me.' In the same way he took the cup also, after supper, saying, 'This cup is the new covenant in my blood. Do this, as often as you drink it, in remembrance of me.' For as often as you eat this bread and drink the cup, you proclaim the Lord's death until he comes."[45]

Presence between betrayal and denial

How remarkable, indeed, that Jesus gives us his body and blood—not in a moment of transfiguration or during that triumphal entry into Jerusalem, but at the very moment he is facing the *betrayal*[46] and *denial*[47] of those closest to him. Jesus declares a new presence, a new reaching out, and a new way of touching people in their need for strengthening faith. The Gospel writers present Jesus as giving this gift of presence at the Last Supper between the revelation of a betrayal and a denial. The Gospel of John does not make mention of either the rite or words of institution but, rather, focuses on the actions that flow from it—namely, the washing of the disciples' feet. (See John 13:21–38.) It is after this remarkable action and teaching that Jesus foretells the betrayal and denial.

The first Christians repeated and celebrated this *doing in remembrance of me* or *breaking of bread* in the context of a meal. By AD 155 we have a clear witness for the order of the Eucharistic celebration. Justin wrote to the pagan emperor Antoninus Pius explaining what Christians did.

> *On the day we call the day of the sun, all who dwell in the city or country gather in the same place.*
>
> *The memoirs of the apostles and the writings of the prophets are read, as much as time permits.*
>
> *When the reader has finished, he who presides over those gathered admonishes and challenges them to imitate these beautiful things.*
>
> *Then we all rise together and offer prayers for ourselves…and for all others, wherever they may be, so that we may be found righteous by our life and actions, and faithful to the commandments, so as to obtain eternal salvation.*
>
> *When the prayers are concluded we exchange the kiss [of peace].*
>
> *Then someone brings bread and a cup of water and wine mixed together to him who presides over the brethren.*
>
> *He takes them and offers praise and glory to the Father of the universe, through the name of the Son and of the Holy Spirit and for a*

considerable time he gives thanks (in Greek: eucharistian) that we have been judged worthy of these gifts.

When he has concluded the prayers and thanksgivings, all present give voice to an acclamation by saying: "Amen."

When he who presides has given thanks and the people have responded, those whom we call deacons give to those present the "eucharisted" bread, wine, and water and take them to those who are absent.[48]

This *breaking of bread* has taken other names through the years—names that signify some aspect of what the church calls the Sacrament of Eucharist.[49]

As the Son of God becomes incarnate in Mary by the overshadowing of the Holy Spirit, so the risen Christ becomes really present and incarnate by the words Jesus spoke at the Last Supper and the invocation of the Holy Spirit. This real presence, this reaching out, this touching, this nourishing, this Eucharist is "the fount and apex [the source and summit] of the whole Christian life" (Lumen Gentium—11).[50] Jesus is true to his word that he will not leave the disciples or us orphans. That is not just a nice thought. It is the reality of what Eucharist means and is. Eucharist is not a static sign. No sacrament is. Rather they are dynamic and empowering signs for those who receive them with the Spirit of faith. "It is your faith that saves you," Jesus says again and again.

Being a presence witness

What the sacraments empower us to do is to become the living sign that we receive so that we might recognize and become a dynamic and empowered witness to the God within.

The *doing and remembering* that Christ envisioned will definitely take us out of our comfort zone, just like it did the disciples at the Last Supper. It was remarkable that Jesus sandwiched the institution of the Eucharist between a foretelling of *a betrayal* and *a denial*. Eucharist happens in real life as does presence, and until we recognize that, Eucharist—for all its potential—remains simply a mystery.

Here's an example of what I mean. St. Justin ended his description of the Eucharistic celebration with the statement that when he who presides has given thanks and the people have responded, those whom we call deacons give to those present the "eucharisted" bread, wine, and water and take them to those who are absent.

Nothing is noted here about reserving the sacrament as such. But we know that the custom of reserving did indeed come about as well as the liturgical rules for reserving the Eucharist. The consecrated Hosts are placed and secured in a tabernacle, which is usually very ornately decorated. And that is as it should be to honor the real presence. The sacrament is then available for adoration and to be taken to the sick if that need arises. And that is good. Catholics will either genuflect or bow before the tabernacle as an acknowledgment of the risen Christ's presence. And that too is very good.

Here is where the sacrament and the real presence get *real* in our lives. If we acknowledge the real presence of the risen Christ in the tabernacle under the appearance of bread, how do we recognize and acknowledge all the other places where the Eucharistic Christ chooses to be present? Even as we receive Eucharist, are we aware of the real presence of the risen Christ in ourselves and in the people who have just received the bread of life along with us—the elderly man or woman moving slowly with a walker or cane, the mother or father struggling to keep children in the line, the teens with multiple body piercings and stylish haircuts and hair color? This challenges us to look at the ways we engage each other in church, leaving church, and being with each other during the week.

The Eucharist does not end with the ritual dismissal at Mass. Rather, the Eucharist continues as we are sent *to announce the Gospel of the Lord* and *to glorify the Lord by our lives.*[51] Through the Eucharist, we are called to do exactly what Jesus asked us to *do and remember* in his name. We are called to intentionally reach out to see, touch and nourish people. This dynamic of being *a faith presence* to our world *is Eucharist.* We become what we receive. That was not only a difficult saying to accept, it was a difficult way of life. That is why some of his disciples no longer walked with him.

Walking with Jesus takes a real commitment. First there must be some understanding of where Jesus is taking us. Then there must be the decision and willingness to follow. Recall that in the Gospel of John that John the Baptist identified Jesus *as the Lamb of God.* When the two disciples heard him say this, they followed Jesus. Turning around, Jesus saw them following and asked, "What do you want?" They said, "Rabbi, where are you staying?" He replied, "Come and you will see."

This *call to follow* is a repetitive and a Eucharistic call. It is recorded nineteen times in the Gospels where the words "come, follow me!" are spoken by Jesus.

Every catechesis used to explain Eucharist spends a great deal of time on various ways we should prepare ourselves to receive the Sacrament worthily. And that is important. But if it stops there, then we are only *consumers*. The Sacrament of the Eucharist is not just about *consuming.*

What is very important, and I daresay more important, is the preparation *to follow* where the receiving of Eucharist leads—where the risen Christ in the Eucharist wishes to lead. "...Whoever does not take up his cross and follow after me is not worthy of me" (Matthew 10:38). Being worthy to receive Eucharist is only a beginning to becoming worthy of the One we receive. That comes from a decision and willingness *to follow*.

There are designated times during the Eucharistic Celebration when the ritual calls for a time of silence. These are relatively short periods of silence and can be easily missed. At the very beginning, we are called to prepare for celebrating these sacred mysteries by calling to mind our sins, and then we observe silence before the opening prayer, between the reading, and after the homily, at the end of the general intercessions, and after Communion. These periods of silence are times that we can personalize our worship. We are sinners and are indebted to God's forgiving love. What do we bring to this prayer of praise? What word(s) stand out for us from the readings and homily? What intentions do we have to add to the ones mentioned? And what is going on in our hearts—which is now the dwelling place of that divine presence?

The Eucharist is about sensing; it is about seeing, listening, speaking, touching, and tasting. As we look around the Eucharistic assembly, whom do we see and how do we see them? The Sacrament of Eucharist is meant to develop in us a Eucharistic way of seeing. The Eucharist is about *real presence,* and this cannot be emphasized enough. It is also about seeing the real presence of the risen Christ present in the world in all the ways that Christ chooses to be present and in all those in whom Christ chooses to be present.

The Sacrament of Eucharist is meant to develop in us a Eucharistic way of *listening*. If we are following Christ, we will be willing and ready to *listen* to our brothers and sisters—not only with our ears, but also with hearts that are nonjudgmental and are not condemning. Then when we speak, if we speak at all, it will be the message that Christ wants them to hear.

The Sacrament of Eucharist is meant to develop in us a Eucharistic way of *speaking*. The Eucharist is about *proclaiming*. If we are following Christ, we will be ready to reach out to touch our brothers and sisters with words and actions of compassion, encouragement, and understanding—and yes, even correction (but always with love).

So preparing to receive the Eucharist is a very important work for us. But preparing to follow Christ by becoming Eucharist for others is the way the Eucharist will take us. We will *taste and see* the goodness of God, for the risen Christ will walk with us on our daily journey as Christ walked with the two disciples on their way to Emmaus and as God did with Adam and Eve in the cool of the evening in the Garden of Eden. When our *faith vision and faith action* are engaged, then Eucharist is more *real* than we could ever imagine because it involves the risen Christ and us. Thus, communion with the Holy One happens and becomes real in us.

± Bringing the Rite to Life ±

The act of knowing and being present

Father Richard Rohr, in his presentation entitled *Eucharist as Touchstone,*[52] brings this point home in a very dynamic way. He said that he believed that the real presence of Christ is in the Eucharist. Now he has come to recognize that the very concept of presence is inherently and necessarily relational. Catholics can defend the doctrine of the real presence all they want, but if they do not teach the children of God how to be *present to presence,* there is no real presence for them! He went on to say that we spent much of our history arguing about *the how* and *the if* and *the who could do it,* instead of simply learning how to *be present* ourselves. We made it into magic to be believed instead of a transformation to be experienced. We emphasized the role of the ordained and much less the role of the people. (Yet even Canon Law always said that the sacraments are *pro populo,* for the sake of the people, and not an end in themselves.)

Searching for and finding real presence

A good way to prepare for Eucharist and reflect on how well we are becoming Eucharist is to read Matthew 25:31–46. Jesus gives us the criteria that will be used at the final judgment. It is not some exotic theological exercise we will be asked to perform. Rather, it is a basically human task that all are able to do, if they choose. It is about noticing others and sharing. What makes these humble human acts so powerful is that we are told that what we do for the least of our brothers and sisters, we do for Christ. When we feed the hungry, give drink to the thirsty, welcome strangers, clothe the naked, care for the sick, and visit those in prison, we minister to the Christ image in them, the Body of Christ.

The taking or consuming of Eucharist is about opening ourselves to receive the risen Christ into our hearts so that we can be transformed and transfigured into the very Body of Christ, which carries out both the corporal and spiritual works of mercy. The apostle Paul really stressed the reality of the Body of Christ that the community of believers is to become. In his letter to the Corinthians, he writes this: "There are different kinds of spiritual gifts but the same Spirit; there are different forms of service but the same Lord; there are different workings but the same God who produces all of them in everyone."

Paul continues as he shows the various gifts that the Spirit bestows on individual members of the community: wisdom, knowledge, healing, prophecy, and others. These gifts are for the good of the whole body—namely, the Body of Christ. The gifts may be as different as the members of the body are different, but their purpose is for the good of all. The gifts are for the unity and peace of the community, not for division and discord. All these unique gifts of the members are of the Spirit, bestowed to bring health to the Body of Christ–the people of God.

Not to move beyond just the routine and ritualistic reception of Eucharist is to make *a mute idol or a noisy gong or a clashing cymbal* of what is a dynamic and empowering work of the Spirit. And that work and ministry will never come alive in those called and chosen to bear witness if it remains simply a routine ritual. Like the Ten Commandments, *chiseled in stone*, they are meaningless until they are *chiseled into flesh* and given life by the people of God.

Here, again, we see the possible sin against the Spirit. The people of God, gifted by the Spirit in a variety of ways, must guard against being caught up in jealousy, shame, a sense of unworthiness, and all the other ways that paralyze the Body of Christ. For some reason it is easier for some to believe and see the risen Christ in the consecrated bread and wine than it is to recognize the same risen Christ in the "Eucharisted" body of the assembly. This can happen when there is a disconnect between the Eucharistic Body of Christ and the people of God (or when a connection was never made in the first place). We need to make this connection intentional between the Eucharistic presence and all the places where Christ chooses to be present, if it is to be meaningful. We must remember it is Christ who does the choosing and establishes the criteria for his presence. We need to remember this to the point where every time I am in the Eucharistic presence in church, I recall that this presence includes all God's people living and dead. And every time I am in the presence of God's people here on earth, or remembering those who have died, Christ is truly present. We do not make this happen; Christ does because Christ has chosen to be present. We are simply learning to become aware of the mind of Christ.

"Do this in memory of me!"

We know that there are things in our lives that we choose to have in order to function in many different ways. When the need is no longer there, we discard these things because they no longer serve a function. Then there are some things that are seemingly no longer functional, but we keep them *in memory of*...and each one of us can fill in the blanks. It might be a photograph or letter, an article of clothing, or a dried rose petal. The item itself becomes valuable because of the meaning we have placed on that item. The keepsake could represent an event or a person. Even though the event or person is in our past, the relationship is not. Even if the item is lost or misplaced, the relationship is not gone until I make the decision to let it go. Jesus's invitation to his disciples to "do this in memory of me" is all about a relationship. The breaking of the bread and the taking of the chalice are actions we are invited to do in memory of Jesus and all in whom Jesus chooses to dwell. And we dare not try to separate the parts of the Body of Christ.

We must allow the Spirit we received in baptism and which confirmed us in faith at confirmation and which makes holy the gifts for consecration in Eucharist to cure us of our blindness and empower us with the faith vision and faith action that makes the body and blood of the risen Christ visibly present in the world. The spirit of Eucharist nourishes our baptismal faith and life. The spirit of Eucharist strengthens our confirmation commitment and lights our way to *following and becoming* Christ.

These three sacraments—baptism, confirmation, and Eucharist—are tightly bound together. Together they initiate us, and they sustain and nourish us throughout our faith-life journey. We receive them within the context of a faith tradition. But they engage us, beckon us, and open us to so much more and so far beyond—namely, into union and communion with God: Creator, Redeemer, and Sanctifier.

The rite of the Sacrament of Eucharist has a place and time. Let us pray that the fruit of the sacrament becomes an integral part of our life now and forever.

Chapter Three

∞ Sacraments of Healing∞

Living with polar opposites

We are born into a world and a life that are very complex. There is so much good, beauty, happiness, and joy. But it seems that the coins of life are two-sided. On the physical sphere of our life, there is health and illness, wealth and poverty, plenty and scarcity. On our spiritual sphere, the coin of goodness can be flipped and reveal its bad side; the coin of beauty, its ugly side; the coin of happiness, its side of sorrow; and joy, its side of depression.

Just as we sustain our physical life in and through the gift of medicine and other forms that promote physical health, so in the life of our spirit, we must bring ourselves to the ways and gifts of healing when weakness and sin threaten our well-being. It is only with the help promised us by God that we can face the mystery of good and evil, grace and sin, health and sickness, and life and death in our spiritual and physical lives.

Two therapeutic forms of healing

The Sacrament of Reconciliation (confession) and the Sacrament of Anointing of the Sick are signs of healing that empower us to be open to being reconciled and reconciling and to embrace our human condition, fragility, and mortality with life-giving hope and perseverance.

These two signs of healing affect both our *spirit life* and our *physical life*. In our current *reality* culture, there is a tendency not to own and face up to our spiritual and physical brokenness. In theory we know that things are not right in the world (violence, terror, poverty, injustice). In theory we know that we will die someday. Practically, we tend to shy away from these thoughts until the circumstances in life get our personal attention.

These two signs of healing are meant to remind us and let us know life's reality so that we can enter into it, be prepared for it, and embrace it so it need not be so traumatic.

Unfortunately, there is an aversion to these two therapeutic forms of healing in most cultures today, especially in highly scientific and technological cultures. Evil tends to be if not relative, then at least expedient, depending on the definer. For example, it is ethnic cleansing only if it is your ethnicity that is being threatened. While global leaders gather often to discuss poverty and hunger, millions of people are starving— not because of natural causes but because of humans perpetrating violence. Feeling helpless and afraid to name the evil, lest they offend, many leaders do little or nothing. If they really had the courage to address poverty and hunger, the threat of terrorism would drop significantly, and the money not needed for the military could go to solving even more of the world's problems. Corporations deny any wrongdoing, but they pay the fine anyway, paying more to attorneys than they do to victims. Politicians pay attention to the poor when it is expedient but do little to help because it might cost them votes. Welfare for the poor is seen as detrimental to the economy while welfare for corporations is seen as beneficial. Over time, this mind-set becomes systemic, institutionalized, and like a cancer, it will need some very serious therapy.

Unrepented wrongdoing

What we have to come to realize is that before evil becomes systemic and institutionalized, it is the result of actions carried out and/or accepted and approved by individuals. And it is there that the therapy must begin. And that can be a very long process. As Myroslav Marynovych said when receiving the Truman-Reagan Award in 2014, "We all had to learn that an evil deed becomes part of the past only when it has been condemned and repented of. Unrepented wrongdoing inevitably serves as a source of new problems."[53]

Therein lies the healing dynamic of forgiveness: name it, own it, and repent of it. Like any physical illness, if we think it's just a cold when it is pneumonia, or a pain when it is a tumor, or a headache when it is an aneurysm, healing is not likely to begin. We are bombarded by commercials that try to alert us to symptoms that can endanger our physical health. Obviously, they want to sell their remedy, but it is a good way to remind people not to take some symptoms for granted. Ignoring them can be dangerous. People would be wise to mention these symptoms to their physician. It is better to be told that the symptoms are nothing to worry about then to be told it's too late to do anything about them.

The same is true of our spiritual health. It is important to have a good sense of what a healthy life of the spirit might be. Like our physical health, symptoms are indicators of something that might be wrong. A pain or a fever or an addiction is such a symptom—so too with our spiritual health. A feeling of shame or guilt or emptiness needs to be tended to. Maybe it is nothing, but then again, it might be an indicator that I need to do something about it. The Sacrament of Reconciliation might be the place to start if we are serious about seeking peace of mind and heart.

The Sacrament of Anointing is the second therapeutic remedy we might need to face the reality of living. Again, there is an element of denying our mortality that is very prominent among people, but especially among the people in the Western culture. With the advances made in medicine, illness can be seen simply as a nuisance where you have to take some medication and then get better. Although most people do not generally think about death itself very much, they obviously are very concerned about any diminishment of youth and appearance. You have only to look at the amount of money that is spent on maintaining a youthful and fit appearance and cosmetic image. This can be healthy as long as it is not in place of or denial of the real self-image.

The timeline of life

When we realistically contemplate the timeline of a person's natural life, it is something like a bell curve—unless the life is cut short for some reason or another. But from the time of one's conception and into our maturing years, life is ever expanding. We go from our mother's womb into her arms. Next we are placed in the small world of a crib and then the larger, but still guarded, world of a playpen. Our life expands to a room or a house, a back yard or a neighborhood, and so forth. There seems to be no limit to where we might go, maybe even into space. Our minds can even take us to places our bodies cannot.

Then there is the moment we come to the top of the curve, and, without really knowing it, our world begins to diminish. Usually this is a subtle process until it picks up speed. Neither our mind nor our body takes us quite as far anymore; and wherever it takes us, it is with greater effort. Then we find ourselves not wanting to leave our neighborhood or our yard, our house or our room. Then our playpen is a recliner or wheelchair. Then, perhaps, our world shrinks to a bed with bars to keep us from falling out.

Father Pierre Teilhard de Chardin in his book *The Divine Milieu* takes up the theme of the timeline of life in a very direct and personal way. Teilhard has given us this prayer:

> *When the signs of age begin to mark my body (and still more when they touch my mind); when the ill that is to diminish me or carry me off strikes from without or is born within me; when the painful moment comes in which I suddenly awaken to the*

fact that I am ill or growing old; and above all at that last moment when I feel I am losing hold of myself and am absolutely passive within the hands of the great unknown forces that have formed me; in all those dark moments, O God, grant that I may understand that it is you who are painfully parting the fibers of my being in order to penetrate to the very marrow of my substance and bear me away within yourself.[54]

It takes a great deal of courage and faith to embrace the reality of life and to put it into perspective. Many people see the downside of the curve when the body, and sometimes the mind, weakens as just a diminishment. There can be an assumption that all this signals a lessening of productivity and usefulness. And in many ways that is how Western society treats its elderly population, and thus, that is how many people see themselves.

The biological sciences have responded in remarkable ways to slow down the physical effects of this diminishment with advances like prosthetics and the growing of human body parts in laboratories. Amazing strides in dealing with cases involving veterans have been made to the point where, after having suffered traumatic injuries, veterans are able to recover various degrees of functioning—both mentally and physically.

There also have been markedly better ways to respond to the needs of the elderly. Atul Gawande[55] has written a marvelous account of some of these efforts as well as pointing out specific changes that are needed in the medical community to better serve our increasingly older population. He especially highlights the mental, psychological, and spiritual needs of the elderly that demand attention and underlines how that positively affects their physical well-being.

In much the same fashion, the Sacrament of Anointing is a countercultural sign of empowerment and of healing. Rather than making invisible and warehousing our sick, infirmed, and elderly brothers and sisters, we invite them into the midst of the faith community so that they know they are supported, prayed for, and respected. We honor them—not only for the life they have lived and with which they struggle, but we honor them for the ways they continue to minister to us and to others by the way they live with their illness and their mortality. The Sacrament of Anointing thus heals the community of its false sense of reality and strengthens us to face life's ultimate issues.

∞ Sacrament of Reconciliation∞

*Forgiveness is the greatest gift
we can bestow on each other.
No one can give it for us.
It is the seedbed for growing peace
and our only path to freedom.*

Forgiveness—the greatest gift

William Barclay in his *New Testament Commentary*[56] gives us a remarkable statement on reconciliation. "Jesus said many wonderful things, but rarely anything more wonderful than, 'Father, forgive them, for they know not what they do.'" Christian forgiveness is an amazing thing. When Stephen was being stoned to death, he too prayed, "Lord, do not hold this sin against them."

There is nothing as awesome and rare as forgiveness. When the unforgiving spirit is threatening to turn our hearts to bitterness, we need to hear again our Lord asking forgiveness for those who crucified him. Paul picks up this theme, saying to his friends, "Be kind to one another, tender-hearted, forgiving one another, as God in Christ forgave you" (Ephesians 4:32).

Peter said to the people, "I know that you acted in ignorance" (Acts 3:17). Paul said that they crucified Jesus because they did not know him (Acts 13:27). Marcus Aurelius, the great Roman emperor and Stoic saint, used to say to himself every morning, "Today you will meet all kinds of unpleasant people; they will hurt you, and injure you, and insult you; but you cannot live like that; you know better, for you are a [person] in whom the spirit of God dwells. Others may have in their hearts the unforgiving spirit, others may sin in ignorance; but we know better. We are Christ's disciples; and we must forgive as he forgave."

Jesus not only asks God to forgive them, Jesus also gave them an excuse: "Father, forgive them, for they know not what they do." (Forgive them, for they forgot who you are and who they are.) When we do not remember who we are, namely the children of a loving and saving God, we tend to try to do things on our own. Often in the retelling of our family-of-God story, important parts of the faith are then lost.

And so it begins—sin, that is

In the book of Genesis, the human struggle to be like God—as depicted in Adam and Eve—knowing good and evil, is a good example. Adam and Eve did not have to eat of the tree in the middle of the garden. They did not have to try to be like God. They must have already forgotten that they were created in the image and likeness of God. Then when God came looking for them, they hid, for they were naked. In their shame they sewed fig leaves together to cover up their nakedness. Ah, humans—some things never seem to change even after all these years.

Then there is the story of Cain and Abel in which God asks Cain where his brother is. Cain, in another attempt of covering up, then asks God the question that has echoed down the ages, "Am I my brother's keeper?"

From the very beginning, we come face-to-face with the reality of how we were created to live what Jesus calls the "Two Great Commandments," loving God above all and our neighbor as ourselves. And when we fail to do that, we fall into *spiritual dementia and schizophrenia*: We forget the *real* and try to make *something unreal* into *something real* and end up embracing that. Then we wonder why we are not happy, satisfied, and fulfilled.

The price of forgetting

Jesus came to cure us and all people of this *dementia and schizophrenia* and to remind us and all people who God really is and who we really are. He also came to show us the unreality of our attempts to fashion a god in our own image and likeness. This effort on the part of Jesus resulted in his crucifixion and death. People preferred a god of their own creation and were not too interested in being their brothers' (or sisters') keepers.

What looked like absolute chaos, defeat, and a dead end on the cross, through the Spirit of God, became the occasion for a new creation, victory, and an open-ended source of grace and revelation of God's never-ending love. It sustains us in the promise and covenant of God into which we are baptized, confirmed, and nourished. For when we come to recognize our own dementia and schizophrenia and own them, God is ready to forgive and forgive and forgive, *seventy times seven.*

The letter to the Hebrews underlines this forgiveness and ties it to Eucharist and covenant.

> *Every priest stands daily at his ministry, offering frequently those same sacrifices that can never take away sins. But this one offered one sacrifice for sins and took his seat forever at the right hand of God; now he waits until his enemies are made his footstool. For by one offering he has made perfect forever those who are being consecrated. The Holy Spirit also testifies to us, for after saying: "This is the covenant I will establish with them after those days, says the Lord: 'I will put my laws in their hearts, and I will write them upon their minds,'" he also says: "Their sins and their evildoing I will remember no more* (Hebrews 10:16–18).[57]

The Sacrament of Reconciliation is the sign by which we can actively enter this dynamic of forgiveness with which God embraces us. It is a moment in time in which we recognize the actions and attitudes in us that disfigure this *image and likeness of God* that we are. Rather than allowing ourselves to be led by the Spirit of God, we follow the sirens of other spirits into a world of *counterfeit love*—of which we are always the object as well as ultimately the victim. Sin is always a denial of our real selves and thus a denial of the *image of God* that we are. Sin obstructs the flow of *the Life of the Spirit* in us and thus out of us into creation. Sin always and will always be a *lie*.

Whereas sin is the *siren* of so many false spirits calling us to selfish love, the Sacrament of Reconciliation is the *sign* of God's Spirit calling us to a true recognition and love of self.

Jesus relates a parable to illustrate the focus and dynamic of reconciliation.

The way and promise of forgiveness

In the Gospel of Luke we find this comforting statement of Jesus: "Just so, I tell you, there is joy in the presence of the angels of God over one sinner who repents."

Jesus then gives us the parable of the father and the two sons. (See Luke 15:11–32.) Basically, the younger son wants his inheritance now and the freedom to do with it what he chooses. So he leaves his father and older brother (and, I imagine, mother and perhaps sisters) and goes on a spending spree of sorts. However, in his spending without a source of income, his experience of the easy life is short-lived. Life's dilemmas have a way of bringing us to ground. "Coming to his senses," he realizes that he has made a bad choice. So he sets aside some of his pride and heads toward home with the idea that he will apply for the role of servant, and he has his speech all memorized.

> But while he was still far off, his father saw him and was filled with compassion; he ran and put his arms around him and kissed him. Then the son said to him, "Father, I have sinned against heaven and before you; I am no longer worthy to be called your son." But the father said to his slaves, "Quickly! Bring out a robe—the best one—and put it on him; put a ring on his finger and sandals on his feet. And get the fatted calf and kill it, and let us eat and celebrate; for this son of mine was dead and is alive again; he was lost and is found!" And they began to celebrate. (Luke 15:20–24).

Somehow in all his scenarios of what would happen when he returned home, he had not imagined a celebration—at least not a happy one. And for that matter neither has the elder son who happened to be in the field at the time the celebration began.

> *Now [when] his elder son...came and approached the house, he heard music and dancing. He called one of the slaves and asked what was going on. He replied, "Your brother has come, and your father has killed the fatted calf, because he has got him back safe and sound." Then he became angry and refused to go in. His father came out and began to plead with him. But he answered his father, "Listen! For all these years I have been working like a slave for you, and I have never disobeyed your command; yet you have never given me even a young goat so that I might celebrate with my friends. But when this son of yours came back, who has devoured your property with prostitutes, you killed the fatted calf for him!" Then the father said to him, "Son, you are always with me, and all that is mine is yours. But we had to celebrate and rejoice, because this brother of yours was dead and has come to life; he was lost and has been found* (Luke 15:25–32).

We have heard this parable many times. It is used frequently at communal penance services. There are so many points one could stress. But the two key points I wish to reflect on are these: "But when he came to himself..." and "...while he was still far off, his father saw him and was filled with compassion."

Coming to oneself

No matter who the person is or what the person has done, there have to be these two key elements: "coming to oneself" (realizing who we really are and who we have become) and the forgiveness and compassion of the one offended. For a time the younger son forgot or denied the person he was and the relationship he had with his father. The very fact that he asked for his inheritance while the father was still living was a sign that he did not understand or did not accept his relationship to the father except in terms of the inheritance, to which—at this point in time—he was not entitled and certainly did not earn. The fact that he squandered his inheritance was a sign that he could not handle his sought-after freedom. It is the sin of Adam and Eve all over again—unwilling to accept one's relationship with God and unable to handle the gift of freedom God had given.

So the younger son needed to *come to himself* and *come to his senses*. But even in his *coming to his senses*, he still tried to control the situation. By allowing himself to become a victim of not only guilt but also shame, he created a scenario for returning. So he worked out his speech: "Father, I have sinned against heaven and before you; I am no longer worthy to be called your son; treat me like one of your hired hands." He now has come to the understanding that he has sinned. He has not yet come to the understanding of the relationship. He does not trust the love of the father. "Treat me like one of your hired hands." He completely changes the relationship just like Adam did. "I heard the sound of you in the garden, and I was afraid, because I was naked; and I hid myself" (Genesis 3:10). Adam still was not ready to accept God on God's terms, and neither was the son prepared to accept the father as father. They are simply too much tied up in themselves, which is the DNA of every sin.

Forgiveness and compassion rule in this case

But "while he was still far off, his father saw him and was filled with compassion." So the father completely disregards the son's words. Before the prepared speech could be finished, the love of the father took over. In the father's eyes and heart, this was and always would be his child. There's no doubt that the father not only understands the relationship, but he is not about to change it. So the father externally clothes the son in all the symbols of that relationship, hoping that the son will recognize it and take it to heart. "For this son of mine was dead and is alive again; he was lost and is found!" The celebration begins.

In the likeness of Cain

So that takes care of the obvious sinner. But Jesus didn't tell the parable so we could focus on the obvious sinner, namely the younger son. He probably looked around the crowd and saw some eyes critical of the father's compassion and unconditional forgiveness and love. Where was the justice in all this? Well, Jesus hadn't completely finished the parable yet. Luke tells us that Jesus was talking to the Pharisees and scribes—those who knew the law. He knew he would have to deal with the righteous ones; so enters the elder son. He also is *returning* to his father. He returns from the field where he was righteously working and hears the celebration going on and finds out what has happened. "Then he became angry and refused to go in. His father came out and began to plead with him. But he answered his father, 'Listen! For all these years I have been working like a slave for you.'"

So it was not just the younger son who had a problem with the father-son relationship. And even though the elder son stayed home, he was *away* as far as the relationship was concerned, for he saw himself as a *slave*. (Remember the younger son, in his scenario for returning, was going to ask to be accepted as a slave.) The older son had not left. He had stayed home and worked. He did not squander his father's inheritance. Actually, it was to be his inheritance. Remember Luke tells us, *"So he divided his property between them."* The younger son asked for it, but the elder son also received his share of the property.

A family divided

But the elder son still did not understand his father's love. For the elder son, it was still the father's property, and he was a slave—not the son with an inheritance. He did all the right things but for all the wrong reasons. Instead of squandering his father's inheritance, he squandered his father's love for him. He could not see it because he saw himself as a *slave*. As a *slave* he could not even begin to see or understand his father and the father's love and compassion. So they got into this battle of words:

> But when this son of yours came back, who has devoured your property with prostitutes, you killed the fatted calf for him!" Then the father said to him, "Son, you are always with me, and all that is mine is yours. But we had to celebrate and rejoice, because this brother of yours was dead and has come to life; he was lost and has been found.

How difficult it is for the self-righteous to recognize their own sin. They see no need to ask for forgiveness. And this inability to appreciate forgiveness makes it so much more difficult to be forgiving. The elder son did not see himself in any way, shape, or form as his brother's keeper, much less as one to be forgiven.

The mystery of the forgiving process

Jesus began this parable with the statement, "Just so, I tell you, there is joy in the presence of the angels of God over one sinner who repents." Having heard the parable, hopefully people will understand that this is the way things are with God and in God's Kingdom. And so it must be with God's people and their relationships with each other!

Like all the sacraments, the Sacrament of Reconciliation has a certain form or rite and is celebrated in time. Unless we understand the reality to which the sacrament points, the grace and power of the sacrament can be misunderstood and thus greatly diminished. Some ways people refer to this sacrament are to speak of confession or the Sacrament of Penance. Certainly confession and penance are aspects of the sacrament. But reconciliation speaks to healing and strengthening a relationship that has been broken in some way. The healing process does include examining one's conscience, confessing, and penance. But we must keep our focus on the reconciling and healing of our relationship with God and with one another. It is our relationship with God that is the initial focus, and it is the forgiveness of God that is our guarantee. And it is in our conviction that God forgives us that gives us the strength, readiness, and determination to reconcile with one another.

All the elements of the Rite of the Sacrament of Reconciliation are present in the parable that Jesus relates. There is the relationship: father-son; there is the breaking of the relationship by the younger son, demanding and squandering what is not rightfully his yet; coming to some degree of recognition of the sin, even if only in a selfish and imperfect way; taking ownership of his actions; confessing his sin in a deliberate way; and then accepting the penance to help heal the broken relationship.

All the aforementioned parts are probably easily recognized with the exception of the *penance*. It wasn't a series of prayers as such or unrelated actions to perform. The *penance* he had to undergo was to be the son that he was. He had to let go of his *hired-hand* speech and accept the father's embrace, the ring, the clothes, and the celebration. He had to come to a new sense of freedom by accepting that he was beholden to the father, not as a *hired hand* but as a beloved and forgiven child. His former attempts to secure freedom not only did not deliver freedom, but they enslaved and almost destroyed him.

The younger son sinned grievously against his father. It was right out there for everyone to see. We readily recognize that. What is difficult to see is that the elder son also sinned just as grievously against his father, but it was more deadly because it wasn't *out there* for people to see. His sin was festering in his heart. We would never have known his sin had he not, in his anger, refused to go in to the celebration and had he not revealed his anger and rage toward *that son of yours*. He obviously saw himself not as a son but as a *slave*.

"Listen! For all these years I have been working like a slave for you, and I have never disobeyed your command; yet you have never given me even a young goat so that I might celebrate with my friends." How telling that statement is! He, too, had sinned against the father-son relationship. No, he didn't run off and squander the father's money, but he squandered the father's love by his attempts *to work like a slave* to merit some kind of reward. "You have never given me even a young goat so that I might celebrate with my friends." He was trying to earn the love of his father—not as a loving son but as an obedient slave. He was trying to earn his inheritance, which was already his, and he missed his father's love and now resented that love. And that is what hell is like.

The demands of the healing process

The Spirit of God, which we engage in the Sacrament of Reconciliation, sets us on the course for righting our relationship with God and one another. That simply means that we first recognize that we live and move and have our being in the environment of God's forgiveness. It is simply there, like air to us and like water to fish. But to be meaningful and enriching, we need to come to an appreciation and acceptance of the forgiveness God extends to us. It is not something we earn. It is God's love gift to the children of God. But we must come to an understanding of why we need it and intentionally accept it.

What is interesting in the parable of the prodigals is that it is a great study in how something so good can go so wrong— the very dynamic of sin. It also points to the fact that there is something of both brothers in all of us.

The good that is sought by the younger brother is freedom. The good sought by the elder brother was the earned love of his father. We all want our freedom; after all, that is how God created us. God created us in freedom so that we could freely choose to love both the God who made us and to love one another. Love is the only valid currency that God recognizes. One cannot force love; counterfeit love will never satisfy.

The younger brother sought his freedom (his good) in all the wrong things and places. None of these things and places was able to deliver the good he sought. On the contrary, they resulted in taking away the freedom he thought he had.

The elder brother sought the love of his father (his good) in all the wrong ways. He saw his position not as son but as slave. He saw his work effort not as a coworker, but as one who must earn whatever he gets. Rather than looking at what he was accomplishing as part of his inheritance, he ended up resenting it. It was his, but he did not understand the freedom he had to enjoy it.

Both brothers needed to *come to their senses*, admit the lie they were living, and come to an acceptance of the father's forgiveness so that they might find the freedom and the love for which they were searching. We do not know what happened after the celebration. Was there ever a real reconciliation of the brothers toward the father and each other? All Jesus tells us is, "There is joy in the presence of the angels of God over one sinner who repents." The father gave the elder son the reason for the celebration: "But we had to celebrate and rejoice, because this brother of yours was dead and has come to life; he was lost and has been found." So Jesus implies a resurrection theme inherent in reconciling. How open ended that is!

But to get there, we must *come to our senses*. We must examine our lives. We must inspect all the good we have done or seek and expose any lie that might be hidden in our motives. We must own the good and the sin: the good, so that we can engage the spirit of gratitude, and the sin, so that we can engage the spirit of forgiveness. Only by such acknowledgment will we ever come to know ourselves. Only by such acknowledgment will our gratitude for the good have any depth and our sorrow for sin have any sincerity. We *own up to* our goodness not for the sake of being proud or righteous, but for the sake of gratitude. We *own up to* our sin not for the sake of being ashamed and depressed, but for the sake of forgiveness.

The grace and challenge of forgiveness

There is a difference between guilt and shame. We must admit our guilt or else there is nothing to forgive. Wallowing in shame, however, is self-focused and is, thus, a sin of pride and closes the door to the gift of forgiveness. That is why confessing one's sins, as difficult as it is, can be most beneficial. Acknowledging that we are sinners in a general kind of way is like saying that we are just human. It is more like an excuse rather than any kind of commitment to do anything about it. For us, being human must be our road to happiness in this life as well the next. For us, being sinners must become our road to the forgiving love of God in this life and the next. So we must take this confessing both our goodness and our sin seriously, or else we do not move anywhere.

But once we do take it seriously and embrace the grace of gratitude for the good and the grace of forgiveness for the sin, then we can get about doing the good God gives us the strength to do. Allowing ourselves to get caught in the quicksand of fear and shame is a waste of time and energy and a denial of the God who is waiting for us to open ourselves to that forgiving love that will give *joy in the presence of the angels of God*, not to mention healing and new life in our hearts.

Becoming forgivers

There is one more important aspect of the parable that can get lost as we shift back and forth examining the sins of the brothers and trying to see how we fit in the parable. The Sacrament of Reconciliation not only embraces us with God's forgiveness, it does so for a purpose. That purpose is so that we go forth in the power of forgiveness to become like the father in the parable. We are not just called to be receivers of God's forgiveness; we are healed so that we might become healers and ministers of God's forgiveness.

We see this clearly stated in the Gospel of Matthew where the promise and challenge of forgiveness comes with a warning if we do not follow through. Peter asks Jesus how often he should forgive anyone who sins against him. *Would seven times be a good number?* Jesus likes the number seven but multiplies it to seventy-seven times. While the disciples are still trying to absorb this, Jesus explains that, in the Kingdom of God, when someone asks to have debts forgiven, that person had better be ready to forgive the debts owed to him or her by others. If we do not forgive others after having been forgiven so much ourselves, there will be dire consequences.

Jesus makes the same point in the prayer he taught his disciples and us: "...forgive us our trespasses [sins] as we forgive those who trespass [sin] against us..." God's forgiveness is not meant to just make us feel good. God's forgiveness empowers us to deal with the sins committed against us with a love and compassion that reveals the love and compassion of the image of God within us. As people of faith, we receive the Sacrament of Reconciliation like we receive all sacraments—not just as an individual, but as a person of faith joined in the mystical and risen Body of Christ. As with all sacraments, we are called and sent.

"The Grace of the Sacrament is that as we 'receive great mercy, we become great mercy.' Mercy becomes our identity."[58] *We are called* to recognize our sinfulness, called to repentance, and called to recognize forgiveness. *But we are sent* to look for, seek out, and forgive those who sin and injure us. That is how the world and creation will be reconciled and become again a garden graced with original innocence. That was the prayer of Jesus from the cross. It is a prayer we can make our own as we become reconciled and reconcilers.

± Bringing the Rite to Life ±

Corps core values

Growing up and having a father in the United States Marine Corps during World War II, I heard him tell many stories about his time in the marines. All of them were vague references about where he had been and some of the things he had done. It was only much later that he told me about what he did on the islands of Okinawa and Guam and in China. *Once a Marine, always a Marine.*

I mention that as a prelude to the strange twists and turns the idea of being a marine led me through. Shortly before I was ordained, I had asked my spiritual director about the possibility of becoming a marine corps chaplain. He told me that one had to be ordained for five years before such a request would be considered. After five years it did not look like it was going to happen. So the idea slipped into the background.

Fast-forward forty years, and I am retired and living in South Carolina when I get a call from the chaplain at Parris

Island asking if I could help him for a couple of weekends. Shortly afterward I get a call from the chief of chaplains wondering if I would consider being a contract chaplain. I soon realized that I was happy to have had those forty years of experience to bring to this ministry. It was an eye-opening and enriching experience that lasted seven years. The chapel on base had been built the year my father did his basic training there. This and many other connections came to life for me.

But all this is an introduction to focusing on the corps core values. The men and women are trained to embrace a set of values that will form a bedrock of character. I know all the military services have them, but I can only speak on behalf of the marines.

Honor—The quality that guides marines to exemplify the ultimate in ethical and moral behavior.

Courage—The moral, mental, and physical strength to do what is right; to adhere to a higher standard of personal conduct; and to make tough decisions under stress and pressure.

Commitment—The promise and pursuit to complete a worthy goal, objective, or mission.[59]

These three core values are the underpinning for the training and transformation of recruits into marines, who at some point in their service to protect, may be placed in harm's way. Throughout their training they are to use these core values as the source of motivation and apply them to everything they do. These core values become the standard against which they measure their character.

The healing power of positive values

Notice that these three core values are positive attributes. The human spirit must see some positive value in enduring the discipline involved in basic training. Many of the pieces in the basic-training process seem absolutely pointless, redundant, and without merit in and of themselves. This is true also when training for a sport or learning the intricacies of becoming a concert pianist or artist. It takes time and perseverance before the transformation takes hold and the larger purpose is recognized. And we will never really progress until we sense and understand the positive value and meaning of where the individual steps are leading us.

If we are to live in an ever-maturing relationship with God, our neighbors, and ourselves, then we need to embrace some core values that become for us a source of motivation as well as a measure of our progress and character. I would suggest three such values: respect, honor, and integrity.

Webster's first definition of these words is as follows: respect is "to consider worthy of esteem"; honor is "a manifestation of respect"; and integrity is "the state or quality of being complete, undivided...sound." These three values are positive and motivational in their outlook and transforming and healing in their application.

The healing power of respect

There is much talk in many cultures about earning respect, and to a limited degree, there is some truth in the talk. But the truth of the statement is rather fuzzy, to say the least. What is the standard or measure to earn respect? Is it in the eye of the beholder, or could it be a little more objective than that? Do we start with our respect meter set at zero or some other setting? This is a very important question because we only honor what and whom we respect and only to the degree that we respect them.

So to what degree do we respect God, our neighbor, and ourselves? And what do God, our neighbor, and we have to do to earn and maintain our respect? Unfortunately, few people actually give much thought to this presupposition, although it is the criteria out of which we act. And because we do not give much thought to it, we go on our merry way expecting God, neighbors, and even ourselves to do things to earn our respect. Life remains a puzzle for people trying to figure out the complex *meriting system* that humans impose on each other.

The good news that Jesus brought to us was that respect was not only our starting point but also the point that we should try constantly to maintain in all our relationships. Why? Because that is what God does. God respects us totally. God has gifted us with free will. And God respects our choices whether they are good or bad. God does not infringe on the boundary of freedom we have been given. Jesus showed us in so many ways how we should respect one another and not becomes slaves to artificially created human boundaries. Jesus never lost respect for people even though, like the woman caught in adultery, they sinned or, like the lepers, they were considered unclean or like so many who were cured, they were poor or, like Zachaeus and Nicodemus, they were rich or, like the women and children, they had no legal standing or, like the centurion and the Syrophoenician woman, they were foreigners or, like Peter and the other apostles, they made bad decisions. So we should feel quite confident that Jesus respects us whatever our issues are. That should be healing for us, and that is where reconciliation can begin.

Can we even begin to imagine what our world would look like if we could learn to apply the healing power of respect as a *starting point* rather than as *earned points*? How much more freely we could relate to family, friends, and even strangers if we really respected others whose worth is seen because they are children of God and not objects to be used and exploited. Then the slave trade, underpaid-worker system, domestic and ethnic violence, billion-dollar pornography business, drug and sex trafficking, unregulated arms sales, and angry diatribe masking as journalism would slowly wither and fade. Signs of reconciliation would begin to flower all around our environment and us, as the fresh air of respect would replace the pollution of judgment, rage, and selfishness. Let us always remember this basic truth: *once a child of God, always a child of God*. We can always work to overcome the flaws.

The healing power of honor

We need ways to manifest the respect that we have for others. Honor has to do with how we show respect. In what ways do I honor God, my neighbor, and myself? How do I keep holy the Sabbath? How specific and intentional am I in how I honor God? Do I honor God by caring for God's creation? Do I honor God by honoring my neighbor? How do I show honor to myself? It is easy to gloss over those questions without much reflection. But actually many of our issues with others and ourselves could be healed if we took the time to connect the dots: God presence, God presence in others, and God presence in self. This can be a great source of healing and maintaining an attitude of honor. As we honor one, we honor all. In speaking of the judgment of nations, Jesus said, "What you did or did not do for one of these least ones, you did or did not do for me." That includes what we do or do not do for ourselves as well. Our tendency to separate and divide diminishes the power to heal.

We know how uplifting it can be when others honor us with respect. Can we imagine what would happen and how we would feel if we entered our world of relationships with honor, maintained its spirit while there, and left in an honorable way? Are we fearful that others might not reciprocate? Should that make a difference? How important is integrity to us?

The healing power of integrity

Integrity is "the state or quality of being complete, undivided...sound." This speaks to how our body, mind, and spirit think and act as one. It means that we do not hide behind a set of masks and lies. Our body language should not be some pretense, our reasoning should not feed on expediency and rationalization, our spirit should not abide in the land of the minimal, and our boundaries should not be just the letter of the law. There seems to be a natural discomfort, distrust, and even dislike for people who turn out not to be what and who they claim to be. Buyers and consumers are told *to be careful and beware* of products and those who sell them. "If it seems to be too good to be true, it probably is," we are told. We are exposed to actors, actresses, and TV personalities who wear makeup. Election time is filled with speeches and promises through which the electorate has to come to a decision for voting. There is now a very thin, or maybe nonexistent, line in journalism between editorializing and reporting just the facts about events. In so many ways, our world has become a make-believe world where the line between the truth and the made-up is significantly blurred.

It would be a real breath of fresh air if we could presume that people were people of integrity. It would be a joy to go about our daily lives without measuring and weighing every word that we hear spoken and/or left unspoken. It would make life easier not to have to interpret all body language, to see if there is any truth present in what is spoken. It would make things like purchasing items with warranties, signing contracts, reading and understanding medical prescriptions, and banking a real joy, if they did not come with all the small print. Small print, which is supposed to instill trust by covering as many situations as possible, has become a mask for confusion as well as deception and, thus, can lead to more distrust than trust. Distrust has become so systemic in the world that it has become the lens by which people view one another and even themselves.

The healing power of integrity is needed more than ever. The place to begin is with ourselves. It would be so uplifting to our whole being—body, mind, and soul—to be able to look into the mirror and say to the person I see there that I respect and honor that person because he or she is a person of integrity, whose words, actions, and motives are sincere. We do not always succeed, and when we do not, we should be quick to apologize and ask forgiveness. We do not mask our weakness or our sinfulness with makeup just to look strong and sinless. If we can be people of integrity who respect and honor God (as well as God in others and God in self), others (as well as others in God and others in self), and self (as well as self in God and self in others), and then we will find healing in ourselves, and we will become instruments for healing in our world.

The rite of the Sacrament of Reconciliation has a place and time. The fruit of the sacrament becomes an integral part of our life now and forever.

∞Sacrament of the Anointing of the Sick∞

At least two kinds of courage are needed in aging and sickness. The first is the courage to confront the reality of our mortality...The second...is the courage to act on the truth we find.[60]

—Atul Gawande

Life and death struggles—their implications

In the reality of our mortality, we seek life and the things that promise and give life. That tension between our living and our mortality is the greatest single influence in the lives of people. It influences our choices and decisions—sometimes consciously but more often than we realize, not so consciously. We have only known *life*. So death seems such a contradiction to who and what we are. So we try to avoid death and its reminders at all cost. We do that because death is a denial of life as we know it. And if we are anything, we are creatures struggling for life, and life with a certain degree of quality.

Besides physical death itself, there are many indicators of death in life. There is sickness; physical, emotional, and mental disability; feebleness and the gradual restrictions that accompany the aging process. A great deal of personal and social expense is used to ward off these conditions. Great strides have been made in the various fields of medical science to help vaccinate people against disease or to help cure or at least ease suffering. And that is all for the good, as long as its purpose is to promote a healthy lifestyle and not a denial of our basic mortality.

Promoting a healthy lifestyle leads to a quality of life that engages us with the reality of everyday experience. Denying our basic mortality leads us to a life of avoidance, uncertainty, and perhaps even despair, because we are afraid to engage the reality of everyday experience. We are in denial of the dying process that accompanies us all our days here on earth. And if we live in denial of death, we are—consciously or unconsciously—living in denial of the resurrection.

Jesus was well aware of how the body and spirit functioned. Dysfunction in one's body can lead to a dysfunction in one's spirit. It also works the other way. So Jesus, the Incarnate One, the healer, does not go halfway. We see this dynamic of healing spirit and body in the healing of the paralytic.[61]

In all of the healing stories (there are eleven of them), Jesus says, "*Your faith* has saved you" or some similar words. In this story we read, "When Jesus saw *their faith*, he said to the paralytic, 'Son, your sins are forgiven.'" It was the faith of those who carried him to Jesus to which Mark draws our attention and to which he says Jesus responded. Nothing is actually said about the faith disposition of the paralytic in the initial coming to Jesus. Mark and Matthew are underlining the faith of those who carry the sick and care for them.

It is those who care for and carry the sick, both in their hearts and arms, that can bring them out of their isolation and disability and into the healing Spirit of God. Sickness is not just something that affects the individual who is sick and/or disabled. It affects any and all who in some way or another are associated with the sick and/or disabled person. It can affect relationships in so many ways.

People who do not have a healthy understanding of sickness or disabilities tend to withdraw. Sometimes the patient simply doesn't want to be seen in whatever condition they might be. Of course, patients need rest and perhaps clinical isolation if the illness is contagious. But isolation brought about by the patient's pride is not a path to health...nor is society's isolating people so that they are out of sight and out of society's awareness a path to community health. Illness and disabilities are a real part of life and not just a prelude to dying. Nor are they necessarily a diminishing part of life. And until we can integrate health, illness, and dying as a real part of our living, we have condemned ourselves to living in fear and have already diminished our ability to really live.

Dying is not the worst tragedy that can happen to us;
Living without faith or hope is a far greater tragedy.

Life and death struggles—anointing our mortality

So the Sacrament of the Anointing of the Sick (no longer called the Last Rites) tries to give us a real positive and, therefore, healthy view of illness and death.

> *By the sacred anointing of the sick and the prayer*
> *of the priests the whole Church commends those*
> *who are ill to the suffering and glorified Lord, that*
> *he may raise them up and save them. And indeed*
> *she exhorts them to contribute to the good of the*
> *People of God by freely uniting themselves to the*
> *Passion and death of Christ.*[62]

We know illness and suffering have always been among the gravest problems confronted in human life. In illness people experience their powerlessness...limitations...and finitude. Every illness can make us glimpse death. And this can lead to anguish, self-absorption, and sometimes even despair and revolt against God. It can also make people more mature, helping them discern in life what is not essential so that they can turn toward that which is essential. Very often illness provokes a search for God or a return to God or a deepening of our relationship with God.

Father Pierre Teilhard de Chardin in his book *The Divine Milieu* takes up this theme of illness and death in a very direct and personal way:

> *In itself, death is an incurable weakness of corporeal beings, complicated, in our world, by the influence of an original fall. It is the sum and type of all the forces that diminish us, and against which we must fight without being able to hope for a personal, direct, and immediate victory. Now the great victory of the Creator and Redeemer, in the Christian vision, is to have transformed what is in itself a universal power of diminishment and extinction into an essentially life-giving factor. God must, in some way or other, make room for the [God-self], hollowing us out and emptying us, if [God] is finally to penetrate into us. And in order to assimilate us into the [God-self], [God] must break the molecules of our being so as to recast and remodel us. The function of death is to provide the necessary entrance into our inmost selves. It will make us undergo the required dissociation. It will put us into the state organically needed if the divine fire is to descend upon us. And in that way its fatal power to decompose and dissolve will be harnessed to the most sublime operations of life. What was by nature empty and void—a return to bits and pieces—can, in any*

human existence, become fullness and unity in God.[63]

In case Teilhard's explanation seems a little ethereal, perhaps this example might help. As living human beings, we naturally view life from the vantage point of our current circumstances—meaning we are alive on the face of the planet earth. So when we talk about birth and death, it can be restricted and conditioned by our point of view. But what if we were to change the point of view somewhat?

The points of viewing life and death

Let's look at our world view from the point of a fetus coming to full maturity. Everything the fetus knows (and I use the verb "knows" in its widest sense) is the mother's womb where it has been nourished and developed. Now the womb can no longer sustain the unborn, and in the nature of things, the unborn will experience—from our point of view—birth. But from the unborn's point of view, the experience will be a dying experience. All that it has ever known has been the limited environment of the womb of the mother, and it is coming to an end and therefore, from that point of view, is *dying.*

From our point of view, we see it as the *birthing* not the *dying.* Nor would we even consider that the unborn child should stay in what has been its comfort zone. And certainly the mother who will suffer the birthing pain would not wish that on the child or herself. No effort is made to communicate to the unborn or give any assurance that in dying to the only life it knows, the unborn child will have the experience of being born into life as we know it. So we take birth for granted and see it as a source of joy and a beginning of life.

Fast-forward to what we see as the ending of life. We call it death. Again our point of view is from this life. For whatever reason—sickness or a fatal accident or event—life is no longer sustainable in the body. The person is experiencing the process of dying. Those observing see only the *dying*. Where there has been an inability to communicate with the unborn about its new life, our faith in God has given us the ability to receive and communicate the *good news* that the dying is part of the *being born* into new and eternal life. The resurrection of Christ has redefined death not as the end of life, but as the *birthing canal* into everlasting life.

David Baldacci in his bestseller *The Simple Truth*[64] ends the story of the amazing journeys of Rufus Harms and John Fiske with a serious but open-ended reflection on death. Rufus had been framed and ended up in prison for twenty-five years, had lost his brother, and is now a man who has very little. But Rufus had seen himself as the richest man on earth because he had taken the risk to believe in the power of the simple truth that he was innocent and that dying was not the worst thing that can happen.

Fiske looked at the calm face of his friend, Rufus, and envied him. He thought, "How very fine it must be to know for certain that your loved one is in a better place, embraced and held for all time by the phenomenon of unassailable good. So comforting a notion at the precise time you needed to feel it. How often did such timing occur in life? Death as joyous. Death as the beginning. Meaning life was both more and less precious because of it."

Our faith does not take away the pain of dying either for the individual or those who suffer the loss. Rather it gives meaning to the mystery of death and dying. It does not take away the emptiness and loss of a loved one. Rather it helps us to recognize that loss as a sign of the depth of the love that we have for our loved one. With time, that empty place can become a shrine not just to the person's memory but also to that person who is now living in the eternal embrace of God.

The Sacrament of the Anointing of the Sick is able to help the individual who is sick physically or mentally, disabled, elderly, feeble, facing surgery, or suffering from some chronic disability to be open to the revelation and the power of the resurrection in order to strengthen that person in faith as well as to bring comfort as the person experiences illness and suffering. The sacrament is a rite for healing both body and definitely spirit. The healing dynamic usually begins with the healing of the spirit, whereby the person recognizes the reality of being human, fragile, and mortal.

We all know that death is a life event for all of us. But it can take a very long time for it to become personal for the individual. The path to that realization can be filled with fear. The Sacrament of Anointing is meant to strengthen us as we journey with illness; to confirm that we do not walk this path alone; to affirm the fact that a community of believers holds us in their hearts through prayer; to help us open ourselves to God's forgiveness; to encourage us in our cooperation with the gift of medicine and caregivers; and to deliver the *good news* that this life—as much as we should try to continue and preserve it—is heading inevitably toward eternal life. It is a sacrament that can be received as many times as we face sickness and other chronic and disabling experiences in our lives.

Community dynamic of anointing of the sick

Many parishes schedule communal services of the Sacrament of the Anointing of the Sick during the year. This has a twofold purpose. First of all, in the past, the sacrament was usually referred to as "The Last Rites." The sacrament was made available when there was an imminent danger of death.

The sacrament was definitely thought of as a sign of death. Even to suggest its reception put a person in an attitude of fear and perhaps even despair. Even though the Second Vatican Council tried to change that mind-set, it has taken many years— if not decades—to overcome the fear associated with the sacrament.

Care awareness

Help with changing attitudes has come from two unexpected sources. The first source was the *hospice-care movement.* Physician Dame Cicely Saunders first applied the term "hospice" to specialized care for dying patients. She began her work with the terminally ill in 1948 and eventually went on to create the first modern hospice—St. Christopher's Hospice— in a residential suburb of London. She introduced the idea of specialized care for the dying to the United States during a 1963 visit with Yale University. Her lecture—given to medical students, nurses, social workers, and chaplains—about the concept of holistic hospice care included photos of terminally ill cancer patients and their families, showing the dramatic differences before and after the symptom-control care. This lecture launched "...[a] chain of events, which resulted in the development of hospice care as we know it today."[65]

Quality caregiving

At first even physicians reacted negatively to promoting such care for the dying. To acknowledge that a person was terminally ill was considered something of a medical failure. It also meant that the medical community had to develop a way to help patients come to a decision about their own care, especially when the only available care had the effect of reducing the quality of living. After many years of struggle, hospice care has reaped unforeseen benefits. Families have been able to be with loved ones in both a loving and caring way.

Experiencing the final days of a loved one has greatly elevated the quality of life. Hospice caregivers have witnessed terminally ill patients' amazing courage and strength of faith. When they are at home, the patients' spirit can be greatly lifted by the presence of family members—including children, if properly prepared.

The second source has been two legal enactments that allowed handicapped people to get back into the mainstream of living. The 1973 Rehabilitation Act banned discrimination on the basis of disability. The second enactment was the American with Disabilities Act of 1990: an act to establish a clear and comprehensive prohibition of discrimination on the basis of disability.

If this can happen on the physical level, how much more can the spiritual needs of the person be met through the Sacrament of Anointing and Healing? In the communal celebration, it allows a faith community to embrace those who are afflicted in any way to continue to be a vibrant and integral part of the community. The faith family prays for those who are sick, elderly, disabled, or afflicted with addiction or mental illness so that they may experience God's healing care. That healing care begins in the midst of the faith family and the anointing itself. There can be a real sense of caring and concern for people in whatever predicament they may be. They are blessed and sealed with the oil of healing.

Caregiving and witnessing even in illness

However, the dynamic of the sacrament is not one directional. By their willingness to receive the blessing and be sealed with the oil of healing within the community, those who are weak or afflicted become a blessing for the faith family. Those who receive the Sacrament of Anointing in their sickness or disability can be witnesses of strength and a healthy faith to those who are strong and healthy in body. Making the sacrament more available to people who were experiencing various debilitating factors in their lives helped to change the attitudes that people had about receiving it. It also gave people more opportunities to avail themselves of the graces of the sacrament, not the least of which is the community support and concern for them. Communal services also can make the whole assembly of people much more aware and conscious of the personal face of illness and other disabilities in life. It challenges us to do a faith check on what we really believe about this mortal life that we live and the immortal life we have been promised by the risen Christ.

The Sacrament of Anointing of the Sick is essentially about the reality of living, both now and always. It does not deny the realities of illness or death. Rather it asserts that even in our sickness and death, there are the realities of healing and life. It takes a special healing grace and strength of spirit to suffer sickness, whatever the outcome. It takes a great deal of patience, endurance, and humility (all of which are signs of healing) to be a caregiver and also to receive care. It takes a special life-giving faith and courage to look death in the face and allow oneself to be birthed into eternal life.

Believing in the resurrection is not a denial of physical death or a denial of the pain and suffering that accompanies it. It is rather the fullness of faith that what began with the spark of life at baptism—acknowledging each of us as a child of God—enflamed us with the Spirit in confirmation, gave growth to us in and through Eucharist, and healed us of our sinfulness through reconciliation will reach its fullness, through our dying and death, with the God of Life forever. Living with faith in the resurrection, we can live our mortal life with the spirit of freedom and without fear.

± Bringing the Rite to Life ±

In appreciation of health

Healing in our world is both a process and a business. As a process, it is all the ways that the body functions to maintain and recover a certain degree of health. As a business, it is all the ways that those in the field of medicine can assist the body in maintaining and recovering a certain degree of health. There have been tremendous strides made in the medical field through the years and the promise of more to come. This is true not only in the area of physical health but also mental health.

It is easy to take this progress for granted. Adverisements in all the various media inform us about these aids to our health and suggest that we try them if there is a medical need. We can become overwhelmed with all the medical information that is directed at us. We can easily lose sight of the gift of healing itself in the midst of all this. Healing is always personal, and we need to take it personally.

One way we take it personally is with a spirit of gratitude. We acknowledge our gratitude for whatever degree of health we have. We learn to be grateful for the symptoms that alert us to a possible health issue. We are grateful for all the opportunities that are available to us to have a diagnosis, for doctors and nurses, hospitals, staffs, and medical insurance. We are grateful for the support of family and friends. Being aware and being grateful helps us to ward off self-pity on the one hand…and an unwillingness to accept help on the other. Both extremes will complicate any healing and lengthen recovery time.

Another way we take healing personally is working to stay healthy in the first place. Unless one is from another planet, we know the warnings all around us about the unhealthy behavior we need to avoid. Part of the grace of healing helps us avoid such unhealthy behavioral patterns. Another grace of healing is the patience required to withdraw from such unhealthy patterns of behavior. And then there is the grace of perseverance in staying on task. In other words, spiritual healing must accompany our physical and psychological therapies even in minor situations. There are some things for which pills and therapies are not sufficient.

And yet another way we can take healing personally is to do all we can to make sure that health care is available to all persons. We can do that by supporting medical outreach programs financially or volunteering in some way. We can pray for and be intentionally conscious of refugees fleeing their homes because of violence or natural disasters, thus lacking sanitary conditions and perhaps health providers. Being aware and praying for people in such situations will find its way into our prayers of gratitude. We need also to pray for leaders of nations and medical corporations so that they will work to overcome the human and artificial barriers that keep basic health care hostage to political agendas.

Not all healing is physical

We also need to be aware that not all healing is medical or exclusively medical. We can become healers when we visit those who are sick or are simply homebound for any number of reasons. Certainly family, friends, and neighbors who are incapacitated might enjoy having their day enriched by a visit. Conversation, some baked goods, or a favorite dish may have a healing and spirit-lifting effect. If it seems appropriate, bringing children along can have both an uplifting effect on the person as well as gently forming needed awareness on the part of the children that they need not be afraid of people with illness or handicaps.

Just as not all healing is physical, neither is it unidirectional. In so many ways, those who reach out to give care receive the grace of healing in return. No one knows what kind of fruit might be yielded from the seeds of healing planted in children as they learn to deal with people in need of healing. Children need to learn ways of reaching out to other children who might just suffer from shyness or might have more complex issues to deal with in life. Just smiling and being friendly might go a long way to making a classmate feel accepted. When children grow up fearing other children because they have a health condition they do not understand, they tend to become adults who fear people with those health conditions. And that fear can be very unhealthy and in need of healing.

Healing of attitudes

When the paralytic's friends lowered him through the roof and placed him at the feet of Jesus (see Matthew 9:1–8, Mark 2:1–12, and Luke 5:18–26), Matthew wrote that when Jesus saw their faith, he said to the paralytic, "Courage, my child, your sins are forgiven!" It was obvious to all that the man was physically paralyzed. Perhaps something in the eyes of those who lowered him through the roof or in the eyes of the man himself revealed to Jesus that there was something deeper—namely, a spiritual paralysis. So Jesus lifted that burden first, which of course became a distraction for the Pharisees. Then Jesus addressed the physical paralysis.

Jesus always links the physical and spiritual. When he cures, he says, "Your faith has saved you." We are body and spirit, intricately woven into one. Physical paralysis can lead to spiritual paralysis and vice versa. We know that worrying can raise a person's blood pressure. We also know that illness can affect how people relate to God and others around them. It is fairly well proven that many physical ailments are mentally and spiritually connected, if not also caused, to some degree. Therefore, to heal the ailment is simply to manage the symptom and not the cause. A deeper kind of healing is necessary. That was the intention of Jesus. He was not going to return a spiritual paralytic to his friends who carried him and lowered him to Jesus. Nor should we.

We need to begin with ourselves by examining and diagnosing some of our attitudes that seem to paralyze our thinking. And then we need to pray for healing. Our need for healing may be some form of deep-seated prejudice that reacts in a knee-jerk fashion to certain people or situations. And it may not even come to the point of our saying or doing anything. But we know it is there. Praying for healing can help lessen, and perhaps break altogether, the hold an issue has on our thinking. The Sacrament of Reconciliation can help as well. The Sacrament of Reconciliation heals us of sins of commission and omission. It also can heal us of our inclinations to sins of commission and omission.

What is our attitude toward the poor ("if they would just try harder!") or toward the rich ("if they just weren't so greedy!")? What are the things or people that seem to trigger my anger? I may have a reason to be angry. Jesus did, after all. Why am I always reticent around some people and freely verbal around others? Experience may have taught me when to speak and when to hold my tongue. The point is that I need to monitor my attitudes so they do not take over and become my default viewpoint.

Healing relationships

We know that relationships are extremely important. We are in relationship with everything and everyone around us whether we are conscious of it or not. We are enriched by our relationship with family, friends, and even our passing relationships with strangers. Like our attitudes, we need to monitor our relationships so we can be aware of maintenance needs and growth. We know that there can arise issues and differences of opinions that can weaken or threaten a relationship.

One of the stories that has stuck with me through the years was the story a funeral director told me. He received a call from the hospital that a man had died, and the family had asked the hospital to call him to arrange for the funeral. The family consisted of the man's two sons. The first son met with the funeral director and gave him the name of the minister and the date for the funeral and then added that his brother was not welcome to attend. That afternoon the other son met with the funeral director and chose another minister and another day with the same proviso that his brother was not to be present. The funeral director called his lawyer for advice. Since there was no problem with the grave site, the lawyer saw no problem with there being two funeral ceremonies, but it would be legally complicated to have two burials. So there were two ceremonies but only one burial. Major healing was needed for whatever issue(s) separated the brothers.

This kind of brokenness seldom happens all at once. Usually there are smaller problems that do not get resolved and are allowed to fester over time. Bruised relationships hurt at the touch and, like physical bruises, need cold packs and time to heal. Physical wounds need balm and ointments and time as the wound first becomes a scab and then a scar and, hopefully, fades. Wounded relationships need the balm of forgiveness and the ointment of forgiving to make the healing process work. Scab picking and focusing on the scar intensifies the wound, which will never heal or fade as long as we keep picking at it.

Sometimes the bruising and the wounding can just seem overwhelming, and, no matter what, there just isn't the motivation or willingness to heal and forgive—the message of healing and forgiveness from the Gospels notwithstanding. We feel like we just do not know how to apply the ointment of forgiveness. Perhaps we are afraid what the healing of this relationship might mean. People who have been physically ill or handicapped for a long time find that they have learned to live with the illness and the handicap. The possibility of being healed brings with it some real fears for them. They have received a certain amount of attention that they will no longer have if they become healthier. Some of the reasons for not doing things will fade. They will be more responsible for things for their daily life. They have found some pleasure in being dependent. And that is fine when people are ill or handicapped. But it becomes pathological when it is the reason they refuse therapies that can help them become healthier.

The same is true for spiritual healing and remedies for the spirit. When we find ourselves in this predicament, then perhaps it would help to step back and just pray for the strength to at least want to be healthy—in this case to want to forgive. Forgiveness is not a feeling; it is a decision we make. We may never come to the point when we feel like forgiving; the wound is just too deep. Then perhaps, like Jesus, we may have to endure the scars and wounds while trying to find it in our hearts to pray, "I want and I choose to forgive" and thus heal and be healed.

The rite of the Sacrament of Anointing has a place and time. Let us pray that the fruit of the sacrament becomes an integral part of our life now and forever.

Chapter Four

∞Sacraments of Shepherding God's People∞

As we listen to Jesus's images and examples, it appears that [the reign of God] is the world of house and field and job and marriage where we are converted to right relationship. The secular has become the place where we encounter the True Sacred.[66]

—Richard Rohr

The ministry of shepherding

The work of both the domestic and liturgical church is all about shepherding, caring, and witnessing in such a way as to make the plan of Jesus for a New World Order visible and viable. The liturgical church is in service to the domestic church, which is in service to the world. The domestic church gathers as liturgical church to be nourished and empowered by the Word and sacrament and then *missioned* anew each time. "Go and announce the Gospel of the Lord." "Go in peace, glorifying the Lord by your life." "Go forth, the Mass is ended."[67]

Whereas the Sacraments of Initiation and Healing minister primarily to the individual through the community, the Sacraments of Holy Marriage and Holy Orders minister primarily to the community through individuals who choose to be bound by a covenant of love—shepherding the domestic and liturgical church.

The domestic church—marriage and Genesis

There are two creation narratives in the book of Genesis. Each account ends with God creating humankind.

> Then God said, "Let us make humankind in our image, according to our likeness; and let them have dominion over the fish of the sea, and over the birds of the air, and over the cattle, and over all the wild animals of the earth, and over every creeping thing upon the earth." So God created humankind in his image, in the image of God he created them; male and female he created them. God blessed them, and God said to them, "Be fruitful and multiply, and fill the earth and subdue it; and have dominion over the fish of the sea and over the birds of the air and over every living thing that moves upon the earth" (Genesis 1:26–28).[68]

> ...for Adam there was not found a helper. So the Lord God caused a deep sleep to fall upon the man, and he slept; then he took one of his ribs and closed up its place with flesh. And the rib that the Lord God had taken from the man he made into a woman and brought her to the man. Then the man said, "This at last is bone of my bones and flesh of my flesh; this one shall be called Woman, for out of Man this one was taken." Therefore a man leaves his father and his mother and clings to his wife, and they become one flesh (Genesis 2:20b–24).[69]

The first narrative gives us the revelation that "God created humankind in [God's] image, in the image of God, [God] created them." God created them "male and female." Then God blessed them: "be fruitful and multiply..."

The second narrative gives us the revelation of inter-action between God and Adam. In the midst of all that had been created, Adam experienced loneliness. So God fulfilled that need by creating *woman* from the very substance of *adamah, man.* God then brought woman to the man so that the man might recognize his own very substance in woman. It is because of this recognition that "a man leaves father and mother and clings to his wife, and they become one flesh."

In the creation story, it is important to note that before they become *one flesh* we are told that they are made *in the image and likeness of God,* that they are male and female made of the same substance—and therefore equal in the sight of God—and that they have received a blessing to be fruitful. This recognition will be the basis for the relationship or covenant that we call marriage. And marriage will be the framework and foundation for family, and family for society. *Flesh* alone would not be strong enough to accomplish that.

The liturgical church—Jesus and his plan for continuing his ministry

> *Now the eleven disciples went to Galilee, to the mountain to which Jesus had directed them. When they saw him, they worshiped him; but some doubted. And Jesus came and said to them, "All authority in heaven and on earth has been given to me. Go therefore and make disciples of all nations, baptizing them in the name of the Father and of the Son and of the Holy Spirit, and teaching them to obey everything that I have commanded you. And remember, I am with you always, to the end of the age. (Matthew 28:16–20).*[70]

"Holy Orders is the sacrament through which the mission entrusted by Christ to his apostles continues to be exercised in the Church until the end of time: thus it is the sacrament of apostolic ministry."[71]

There is a story about what happened right after Jesus ascended into heaven. Our Lord is meeting with some angels and they ask Jesus, "What about your kingdom on earth now? What is your plan?" They were looking down on earth and watching Jesus's disciples, who were dazed and meandering back to Jerusalem to confront the Herodians, the Roman Empire, and the power and principalities of the world. "Well, I have my disciples," Jesus said. "But what if they fail you? What is your plan, then?" Jesus said, "I have no other plan."

Matthew tells us that some of the eleven disciples still had doubts. He doesn't say precisely what their doubts were. Perhaps they still doubted the report of the women who were commissioned by Jesus at the tomb: "Do not be afraid; go and tell my brothers to go to Galilee; there they will see me" (Matthew 28:10). Perhaps the report of the guards (Matthew 28:11–15) created some doubts in their minds. Perhaps, given their behavior over the last few days, they doubted their own ability to do what Jesus was commissioning them to do: "…to make disciples of all nations" (Matthew 28:19).

But Jesus trusts that as his disciples come to understand and experience the Kingdom of God more fully in their own personal lives and as they are empowered by the Spirit, their hearts will be so afire with the good news that they can't help but proclaim that good news. For this to happen, the disciples must come to know the working of the Advocate, the Holy Spirit, that Jesus promised. As we see from scripture, the Holy Spirit is ever present and ever working in both the domestic church (the house of Cornelius) and the liturgical church (the house of Peter).

∞ Sacrament of Holy Marriage:

Love-Covenant Shepherding the Home ∞

Called and sent to proclaim and live the original blessing/command

> *So God created humankind in his image,in the image of God he created them;male and female he created them.God blessed them, and God said to them,"Be fruitful and multiply, and fill the earth and subdue it.*
> (Genesis 1:27–28).

Marriage—human and divine love

There's a flavor of heaven about a wedding. At that moment two people love each other so much that they are prepared to give their lives to and for each other. That is God's kind of generosity—a love that is beyond reason, longer than life, and stronger than death.

Rev. William A. Anderson tells a story that speaks to the mystery and depth of faith and love in marriage in his revised book *In His Light.*

> Marie sat at the kitchen table, speaking with her mother about plans for the anniversary celebration. In only three months, Marie's mother and father would celebrate fifty years of marriage. While they talked, Marie noticed her mother relaxed just a slight bit when she heard the front door open and knew her husband had returned from his daily walk in the park.

Marie reflected on the silent communication that existed between her mother and father after all these years of marriage. Sometimes she would notice a slight tension while she spoke with her father in the living room, especially if the kitchen seemed too silent for too long. But the sound of a pan banging in the sink would ease the tension as she noticed that same light relaxation with her father. She had learned of the concern that existed between her parents for each other, and how the sound of the door opening or a pan banging in the sink communicated that all was well. Through fifty years of struggling, adapting, and even arguing with one another, the two had gradually welded into one.[72]

At the anniversary celebration, the four children, ten grandchildren, and the eight great-grand-children stood as a living reminder of what this marriage had brought to the world. Through her parents' love and their family, Marie was able to understand the ideal of marriage in God's creation. She smiled as she whispered to herself, "I guess God does know what he's doing."[73]

We are a society that speaks more often than not of *young love* with all the excitement that might convey. But what about that love that has stood the test of time: both the good times and the bad. When we witness an elderly couple kissing each other with gentleness and love, we stand in the presence of the sacred. We are touched by the realization that such love elevates human life in solemn beauty.

Now we can better understand why Jesus chose marriage as the sacrament to reflect God's love for the people. We know that some marriages fail and that building a marriage and a family is difficult. But that is precisely what underscores the greatness of this sacrament.

Human intimacy—strength and weakness

The problem with human intimacy, but also the source of its strength, is that it involves an immense amount of risk. In marriage a couple is called to set aside their defenses, their fears, and their little neurotic ways of keeping people at a distance. Intimacy cannot exist without allowing ourselves to become vulnerable. We can only be intimate with someone to whom we have given the power to break our hearts. But it is precisely at this same point where we can only know true love and true happiness.

Where a couple will be in the years following their wedding day, no one can say. But if each day, in one way or the other, they proclaim from their heart, "Honey, you are beautiful and wonderful, and I love you" and "Honey, you are handsome and wonderful, and I love you," then nothing—not poverty, not sickness, not even death itself—will diminish their love for each other and, therefore, their happiness will be of God and it will be without end.

Marriage—struggling to understand

Throughout history, humans have had a difficult time defining what form marriage should take. There are marriage contracts. There are common-law marriages. There are marriages of convenience. There are arranged marriages. There are marriages that give royal entitlements. There are marriages that have been monogamist and polygamist. The role of husband and wife in marriages has been quite diverse also. In some eras and cultures, the bride and the groom have no choice at all, as parents arrange the marriage. In many cultures women have been seen as the property first of the father and then of the husband and have no real or legal standing in society. And even in our time, when given the freedom to choose their respective spouses, couples must tread the dangerous waters of uncertainty—created by the prevalence of separation and divorce in society and also by a confusion regarding so-called free sex as distinct from committed sexuality. A lot of time, money, and effort are spent on being able to act out sexually, and little thought, if any, is being invested as to why one acts out sexually in the first place. That is generally learned through trial, error, and much pain and disappointment.

This inability, failure, or refusal to recognize those three elements in the relationship of marriage (that the husband and wife are *made in the image and likeness of God*; that they are male and female made of the same substance and, therefore, equal in the sight of God; and that they have received a blessing to be fruitful) have made for a clouding or even loss of the vision of who we are, a return to de facto inequality, and a lack of respect for what it means to *become one flesh*. The result of this lack of understanding leads to much suffering and a return to loneliness for couples, families, and societies. The reality of that truth continues to be denied in many ways to the detriment of families in particular and societies in general.

Marriage and the faith dynamic

For the person of faith, it is the recognition of the God image, the love-image, and the life-image blended together in the covenant of marriage that gives the best model to see and experience the creating, redeeming, and sanctifying love of God. For those who are willing to enter into a covenantal relationship, the Sacrament of Marriage offers an opportunity to grow in and give witness to their love before God in the midst of family and friends.

Marriage, like so many human endeavors and life itself, is always a growing experience and one that is lived in tension. A great deal of the tension is caused by freedom itself. The young move in and out of friendships for many reasons and circumstances in their lives, some of which they can control and some of which they cannot. As the prospect of marriage becomes real, the difficult task of choosing needs to be made if that deeper relationship is to come alive and thrive in any way. And when some choices are embraced, other options become a choice no longer. Some people think that as choices are no longer available, their freedom is limited. They do not realize that actually the opposite is true. A person can experience more freedom as the options fade out of the picture. For example, as long as a person stands in the middle of a paint store looking at all the options, the house or the wall or the canvas will not get painted. Once the choices are made, then and only then will the person be free to paint.

Also, if we focus only on what we give up to attain some goal, we may never get there, and if we should mysteriously get there, it would hardly be an enjoyable journey. On the other hand, once we embrace a goal, we focus on it, and the things we give up actually give us the freedom we need to obtain whatever it is for which we are striving.

So the question becomes, "What precisely is the reason a person chooses to marry?" As simple as that question is, the response is as complex and multifaceted as there are people who marry. As mentioned above, marriages begin for many reasons, and experience has shown us that they end for many reasons. But the ones that endure show some common elements that help the marriage begin and grow and then survive the *post-honeymoon years* and the *seven-year-itch years*, the *making-a-living years*, the *emptying-nest years*, the *empty-nest years*, and the *just-the-two-of-us-again years*.

Marriage—The mutual choosing of an *other* for the *other*

Whatever the initial reasons or circumstances for marrying another happen to be (and history has produced a wide range of reasons, from arranged weddings, shotgun weddings, status weddings, and weddings of convenience to "I can change him (or her)" weddings), eventually, if it is to endure, the couple must come to a loving and free, intentional choice of each other. It is this free, intentional love that defines the elements that hold, nourish, and bind the relationship. In a family, parents—even though they biologically give birth to a child—must at some point intentionally embrace the child as their own in an ongoing way; and a child—even though the child is the biological offspring of the parents—must at some point intentionally embrace the parents in an ongoing way. In the same way, a married couple—given all the excitement of young love—must continue to grow in their marriage commitment in an ongoing and deepening way as they grow older.

Paul, in his first letter to the Corinthians,[74] gives us the elements that define the kind of love that nourishes and supports couples in the committed love of marriage—a love that not only does not age but that is eternal. At first glance, this seems an almost impossible, if not impossible, task. But there is an amazing power inherent in love, and it is this: as we grow in love, it becomes its own source of strength and its own reward. It is love that holds a couple together in the face of a devastating illness. In so many other situations, it is love that binds a couple as they face perhaps economic problems, addiction, the loss of a child, infidelity, and other hardships. Many times it is the extraordinary love of one spouse that holds and supports the other, who may not be able to bring him or herself to love to the same degree. That is the amazing thing about love; it is limited only to the degree and extent that the one who loves wishes to limit it. That is the reason that, although seeming to be equal, some marriages fail while others do not. It is the *love factor* that is the grace and power of the covenant of marriage.

The bride and groom are the ministers of this covenant, or sacrament, to each other not only on the day of the wedding; they continue to minister to each other every day throughout their married life. Each ministers to the other as one made in the image and likeness of God, male and female, equal in substance, and blessed by God as they become a blessing for each other. Their becoming one flesh is the confirming sign of their commitment. This confirming sign is always life-giving: it gives life to their unity of love, and it may beget a new and unique life of its own.

A wedding is a radical event

As casually as society seems to take it, a wedding is a most radical event. Usually we think of it as the most natural step in a series of steps toward marriage. But as natural as it may seem, it signals a radical change.

Several years ago I had the opportunity to visit Morocco. After a dinner one evening, they chose a couple from our tour group and enacted a part of the marriage ceremony according to their Berber custom. Here's what they did. They had what looked like a nicely decorated, round tray about five feet in diameter with handles. They placed the tray on the floor and invited the bride to sit in the middle of the tray. Four men then lifted the tray with the bride on it and placed it on the shoulders of four women. Then, very slowly, they turned in place so the bride could see all the invited guests. After a full turn, they stopped for a moment. Then they turned a second time.

They explained that the first turn is for the bride to see and to remember those who were a part of her life up to this moment. As the first turn is completed, there are cries of sadness from many of the guests because that part of her life is complete—never to be repeated. All relationships that were will never be the same. Then, as the bride turns the second time, she sees her future and all the people who will be a part of her life but in a new way. The difference is the marriage. Her whole life and that of her husband will now be centered in the marriage to which they have just vowed themselves, and it radically changes everything. Basic relationships like parent and child, brothers and sisters, and friends will all be configured differently. They have to be if the marriage is to survive.

Even though parents say they want what's best for their son or daughter, it can still be difficult to entrust a child to another. This is true for friends as well. Friends can no longer claim the same kind of time they used to. It takes a while for everyone to get used to the new way of being.

The groom's party and the bride's party are usually made up of friends and relatives who are very special to them. But they will leave the place where the wedding is held differently than when they came in. As the bride is the last one in, she and the groom will be the first ones out. And it will now be that relationship to which all other relationships will be configured.

These things seem so obvious, but in many ways they are life changing. Marriage is a leap of faith. It is not a thing of reason. This couple is entering into a mystery far beyond them. Love is the only vehicle that can transport them there safely. Hope is the only thing that can fuel their journey. Faith is the only thing that can give their journey direction. It is a God thing—nothing more and nothing less.

Marriage and mission

It is said that the world sings when two people, with faces aglow with love, look into each other's eyes and say before God and friends: "We love and trust each other so much that with heaven's grace and the help of family and friends, we will live together, walk together, learn together, and share together, until one of us places the other in the arms of God."

Weddings generally happen in communal settings and rightly so. If it "takes a village to raise a child," it takes a faith community to help and sustain a couple as they begin their married life. All weddings entail at least two crises—one before the wedding itself and one afterward. Anyone who has planned a wedding or helped someone else knows the nature of the first crisis. A thousand and one details must come together at the same time in an almost seamless fabric of picking out dresses and tuxedos, rehearsal, guest lists, and invitations. This process looms initially as an insuperable crisis until the words "I do" are repeated. What had been a crisis becomes an explosion of rhythm, melody, color, food, and drink. Such merriment not only marks the end of the first crisis, but it also signals the beginning of the next. And it may not be recognized until weeks, months, or years later.

The parable of the wedding of Cana[75] reveals to us the nature of the second crisis. The parable begins at the wedding feast. The wedding couple has surpassed the first crisis only to find themselves in another: the wine has run out.

How many couples after ten or twenty years of marriage suddenly feel the feast come to an end? At that point, neither partner feels he or she has much to give and neither feels like trying and the marriage may die. They have no more wine. Such is the nature of the second crisis of weddings. Fortunately, the couple is not left alone to confront the crisis. Cana reveals to us the concern God has for the love between man and woman—to the extent that he allowed his son to depart from his own plans and be persuaded by his mother's urging to change the water into wine. Changing water into wine, however, was not the real miracle at Cana. The real miracle was that the wine was better at the end than at the beginning. Such is the nature of marriage when the love of God is invited to be a part of the marriage.

The miracle of Cana will take place for married couples sometime in the future as they face life with all its mystery and anxiety—and thus the opportunities life brings. And when it seems that the wine has run out, we pray that there will be compassionate people like Mary who suggests that the Lord's presence be recognized and that what seems to be plain water will become the exhilarating wine of their marriage. The miracle will not be the changing of the ordinary into the extraordinary, but rather it will be that the wine of the ordinary things a couple does for each other in the future will be even better than the extraordinary things they do for each other now. For God wishes no less for them than God wished for the couple affected through Jesus's miracle at Cana.

Marriage and community

The Sacrament of Marriage is about celebrating three love stories. The first is the obvious love story: the story of love that the couple has for each other. The second story is about the love that brings family and friends to the ceremony. For the most part, it is the love of family and friends shown to the couple over the years that gives the couple the courage to take this risk of a love promise. By their presence at the ceremony, family and friends are committing themselves to continue loving the couple into the future. The third story of love is the ancient love story. It is the story of the love that God has for all of us. The love of God is a love without condition. It is a love that forgives. It is a love that does not depend on the emotions of the moment. It is the love that we are invited to imitate. A wedding is not just about the couple. Just as no individual person is an island unto oneself, neither is an individual couple. It takes quality love to empower a couple to take the risk of promising love into an unknown future. It is this kind of love that is necessary in order that a marriage can persevere. And, above all, it is the marital love that models and gives witness to the unconditional love of God.

That is why it is good that at weddings the couple comes in the presence of family and friends to publicly proclaim that they are willing to risk making a promise that for better or worse, for richer, for poorer, in sickness and health, until death, they commit their lives to each other. What a blessing for the community to be able to witness this. What a bolster to the couple's faith that the love they have received from their family and friends now bears fruit in that pledge that they give each other. What a sign of hope as they leave their home to create a new home. The community wishes them a long journey together and prays that they be blessed with the gift of compassion: that their words may be words of comfort; their hands, instruments for healing; their home, a place of happiness; and their lives, a source of grace for each other.

The miracle of God's gift of marriage is how dynamic and powerful the grace of marriage is, as it not only sustains couples in their love commitment to each other, but also models and ministers quality love to society at large and is the best witness of God's covenant love for each of us.

Dressing for a marriage

We generally know how one dresses for a wedding. If you are the bride or groom, you can go to someone who knows how to blend color, personality, what looks good, and what matches the chosen color motif. Then you start what can be a long search for the right gown, right size, and right price. The groom searches the stores that rent tuxes, gets fitted, and hopes the right things get delivered. Both the bride and groom pray there is no significant weight gain or loss. Much goes into getting dressed for this one special day.

But how does one dress for a marriage? What are you going to wear to ensure that your marriage will be enduring and satisfying? Paul has some suggestions for a marriage wardrobe.

> *As God's chosen ones, holy and beloved, clothe yourselves with compassion, kindness, humility, meekness, and patience. Bear with one another and, if anyone has a complaint against another, forgive each other; just as the Lord has forgiven you, so you also must forgive. Above all, clothe yourselves with love, which binds everything together in perfect harmony. And let the peace of Christ rule in your hearts, to which indeed you were called in the one body. And be thankful.* (Colossians 3:12–15).

These clothes Paul invites us to put on are not made of natural fibers but are woven of spiritual fibers. They are clothes of the heart, and only those who have the Spirit of Jesus Christ can really put them on. Try as we might in our own power to create them, they run counter to our human nature. Compassion, humility, kindness, gentleness, forgiveness, and love—these do not come naturally. They are gifts of the Spirit of God that we celebrated in the Sacrament of Confirmation and are given to us whenever we prayerfully ask for them.

The first is a two-piece garment: compassion. This spiritual garment has to do with each having the other at heart.

With the garment of compassion, one must put on kindness. Now there's an article of clothing that can get to be in short supply in a marriage sometimes! After a while, one can really get to know the other's weaknesses and sore spots. Kindness doesn't sweep these under the rug, but when you are clothed with kindness, you will be seeking the other's good as you deal with the weaknesses and sore spots. Kindness is like a healing bandage.

Another item of clothing that does a marriage good is humility. If ever there is an area where pride and the need to be right and the struggle for power occur, it can be in a marriage. Lack of humility can lead to all kinds of power struggles—whether it's a struggle over the checking account, over the kids, or over whose turn it is to do whatever. Humility recognizes the other's equal status and recognizes that each has needs and plans that are equally valid. We can only put on humility when we remember that each of us is an equal-in-God's-eyes child of God.

Then there is patience. The wearing of patience may feel like one is wearing a hair shirt. Each will discover that the other has the capacity to drive one crazy! Whether it's chewing ice cubes or trying to ignore the recycling that needs attention, switching channels constantly with the all-powerful remote control or never allowing enough time to arrive on time—it doesn't matter what the issue is; marriage takes patience.

Another essential garment is a spirit of forbearance and forgiveness. There's a lot that needs to be endured in a marriage—a lot that requires forbearance—and it is a spirit of forgiveness that makes difficult things endurable and maybe even erases them. I could never comprehend the movie Love Story that contained the line, "Love means never having to say you're sorry." Nowhere more than in marriage is it true that love means always being ready to say "I'm sorry" when there is something for which to be sorry. Do not say it to get out of a tight spot. Say it because you know that in no other relationship is the other so vulnerable and so easily hurt. And when the other has asked forgiveness, grant it.

Couples must pray daily to be clothed in these spiritual garments so that when the wedding garments are returned to those who rent tuxes and the gown is cleaned and neatly stored away, you are clothed with the spiritual marriage garments that will keep you warm and rejoicing in each other's presence for years and years and years.

Marriage and love

If you are familiar with the cartoon Peanuts, then you can recognize the interesting relationship between Lucy and Schroeder. Lucy says, "Guess what, Schroeder—if you don't tell me you love me, you know what I'm going to do? I'm going to hold my breath until I pass out." Schroeder, looking up from the piano, informs Lucy that "breath holding in children is an interesting phenomenon. It could indicate a metabolic disorder...a forty-milligram dose of Vitamin B6 twice a day might be helpful—I think that's probably it—you need B6, more bananas, avocado, and beef liver." Lucy—quite dismayed—says, "I ask for love, I get beef liver."

The little story might be humorous if it didn't reflect reality so often. What gets defined as love quite often in the media, in music, and the in movies is oftentimes beef liver and is not love—nor is it satisfying in the long run.

A woman gave one of the most sobering wedding gifts I've ever heard of to her husband on the morning of their wedding. It was a framed, beautiful piece of calligraphy. It is a quote from a memorable scene in Robert Bolt's play about Thomas More, *A Man for All Seasons*.

More is imprisoned in the Tower of London. His daughter Margaret is begging him to yield to the king, swear to the Act of Succession, and return home to his family. More replies, "When a man takes an oath, Meg, he is holding his own self in his hands, like water. And if he opens his fingers then, he needn't hope to find himself again. Some men are not capable of this, but I'd be loathed to think your father one of them."

Oaths, vows, and all those carefully chosen words we say to God and to one another, are scary things. It is awesome to speak them and, almost equally so, to hear them spoken.

But there is a flavor and a fragrance of heaven about saying one's vows. For at that moment, two people love each other so much that they are prepared to give their lives for and to each other. That is God's kind of generosity—a love that is beyond reason, a love that is longer than life, and a love that is stronger than death.

The love that couples pledge to each other is not a feeling. No one can pledge a feeling. The love they are pledging is a decision or, to use the biblical term, a covenant. With great faith they are about to defy time and circumstance and selfishness and proclaim that—whenever, however, whoever—they are for each other, all for each other, now and always.

God knows that this is not an easy gift to give. Great generosity never comes easy or cheap. It is a promise that can be made only in humility and with a cry for help: help from family and friends through their continued caring and love for the couple and help from God who will strengthen them in their love for each other. Marriage is a Sacrament of Shepherding Love.

± Bringing the Rite to Life ±

We are used to thinking that what we give is the same as what we receive, but people who love expecting to be loved are wasting their time. Love is an act of faith, not an exchange.[76]

—Paulo Coelho

Deciding as a couple and as a family

A wedding signals a radical change in how the couple see themselves and how they relate to each other and the world around them. As a married couple, they are more than the sum of their individual parts. They are a new entity entirely. And so they have to see themselves as such. Where before they were accustomed to think primarily as individuals, now they must now think primarily as a couple. Hopefully, that process began during their earlier relationship and engagement. Decision making has to be made in the light of the other. How one spends one's time with friends for recreation and relaxation must include consideration of the other. How holidays are spent with family must be discussed and agreed upon. Nothing should be taken for granted. Even the things that seem obvious should be sounded out, just to make sure each is on the same page. It's simply a sign of respect and consideration that needs to be done.

When the couple starts thinking about raising a family, they have to prepare for another radical change. And the more a couple prepares for the responsibilities that come with starting a family, the more comfortable they will journey into this new entity called family. This also signals a radical change in how the individuals are configured to each other as mother, father, and child. This all seems obvious enough, but if left to chance, strange and painful things can happen to the relationship.

Believe it or not, to some fathers the child can be seen and resented as an intruder as the mother focuses so much of her attention on the child. Fathers can also feel inadequate and so hold back from taking some of the responsibility for caring for the child. After a time, a mother can begin to resent all she has to do and not having the free time she had before. Or she may be overly protective and refuse to let anyone, even the father, help her. All of these patterns of behavior are more or less normal in the first instance, but if they hang around and are not addressed in a healthy way, they can be detrimental. It is critical that the husband and wife, now mother and father, prepare themselves for this second radical change in their marriage.

It is also critical that relations with grandparents be monitored. Time with grandchildren is special for grandparents. If both sets of grandparents live close, visits back and forth may be relatively easy. If one set of grandparents lives close and the other at a distance, then it can be a bit more complicated. So the couple has to agree how to handle the situation.

Solving problems as a couple

Serving as a contract chaplain at the Marine Corps Recruit Depot at Parris Island, South Carolina, for almost eight years was enlightening and enriching in so many ways. But it took some getting used to. Most of my ministry was with the recruits. It took a while to get used to listening to them always referring to themselves in the third person: "This recruit wishes to speak to the chaplain." It seemed more than a little strange to me to hear them referring to themselves in this manner: "This recruit, he..." or "This recruit, she..." For thirteen weeks, a recruit learns not to use the words "I" or "me." And it's not just about words; it is all about identity. Recruit training is about forming men and women who think as a team, as a unit, and as a company. For down the road, their very lives may depend on each other. So this way of thinking has to become second nature and woven into their way of thinking and acting.

Couples enter into marriage without the *assistance* of drill instructors. So the transition from thinking and making decisions for oneself and thinking and making decisions in the context of marriage and family takes time and intentional effort. It is no longer just what I want to do. *The I* must become *we*. The *me* decisions are always in the context of *us*. So the individual has to be intentional and comfortable with transitioning from *I* thinking to *we* thinking. That is a critical measure of love as well as a realization that each has embraced the radical change brought about by marriage. The adoption of *the we* also becomes important not only in decision making, but especially in problem solving. If one spouse thinks that something is just the other spouse's problem, then he or she has the tendency to just let the other spouse deal with it. Or the other spouse says that since it is his or her problem, he or she will deal with it.

The reality is that anything that affects the marriage is an *our* issue. Anything that affects the marriage has to be celebrated, decided, and/or resolved together. Maybe one person will be more involved than the other, but from a decision point of view, it has to be a mutually arrived at decision. There are two reasons for this. One is that deciding together lends support to whatever the decision is. Secondly, it is a sign that the husband and wife honor and respect their commitment to the marriage. And that is true even if the decision is to agree to disagree about something or to give the other person some space for a while. It's important that the decision be mutual and shared if the marriage is to be enriched and strengthened.

Marriage and contemplation

Contemplation is intentionally allowing ourselves to be drawn to or marvel at someone or something. It is allowing ourselves to focus on the beauty or awesomeness of someone or something. Some things just seem to capture our attention, like pictures taken from the Hubble Space Telescope or organisms revealed by a microscope. Newborn infants draw that kind of attention. Parents can spend a great deal of time just looking at their child and marveling at the mystery that is in their arms. They look into the eyes that seem to draw them into some unknown depth. They are awed by the fingers and toes. They muse about what and who this child will become. And this is as it should be. Their love for each other has borne fruit and has taken on a life of its own. The *we* of marriage has become the *we* of family.

Wouldn't it be great if one could hold on to the ability to contemplate one's child through the various stages of growth? In some ways parents do that by taking photos and saving mementos. These are ways of helping parents to keep the contemplation of their children ongoing, even in the midst of the changes and stages that growth brings with it. Some of that focus can get lost when the child begins to move into the more independent years, and discipline becomes more strident. Then it can get tougher to see the qualities of innocence and lovableness at times. But it is important that parents continue to keep their ability to contemplate their children alive through the years. It is also important that parents continue to contemplate each other as they grow older through the various stages of marriage. The wonder and awesomeness is still there in far greater ways, and it would be unfortunate to miss that.

The rite of the Sacrament of Marriage has a place and time. Let us pray that the fruit of the sacrament becomes an integral part of our life now and forever.

∞ Sacrament of Holy Orders:

Love-Covenant Shepherding the Church ∞

Identifying priestly service

Through our baptism we all share in the one priesthood of Jesus Christ, and as such we are called to praise and worship "through...with...and in..." Christ. It is through the priesthood of our baptism that we offer our gifts of service to our brothers and sisters to God in and through Christ. We do this both as individuals and as a community of faith. When we perform loving care to others in service to the Gospel, we act out of the priestly call of our baptism. We bring all those acts of loving service to Eucharist where they are united in the common offering of bread and wine during the time of the ritual offertory. We must be careful not to allow the monetary offering, also done at this time, to deflect the significance of this ritual. The Presentation of the Gifts includes the bread and the wine, as well as the ministries and charitable works done by the people. It is this gift offering that the priest-presider is ordained to pray in the name of all the baptized as follows:

> Therefore, O Lord, we implore you by the same Spirit, graciously make holy these gifts we have brought to you for consecration that they may become the Body and Blood of your Son our Lord Jesus Christ, at whose command we celebrate these mysteries (Eucharistic Prayer III).

As marriage is a *love-covenant* shepherding *the home*, Holy Orders is a *love-covenant* shepherding the *church*. Those who are ordained (bishops, priest-presiders, and deacons) are called forth from the community of the baptized to embrace a love-covenant of service to the people of God. What defines this love-covenant of service is the primacy of God's Word in and through Jesus Christ by the power of the Holy Spirit. Pope Francis, in his address to bishops, speaks pointedly to this love-covenant.

> *When the Lord gives us our mission, he founds (establishes) our being. He does not do so in a merely functional way, like someone who gives someone a job or occupation. Rather he does it with the power of his Spirit, in such a way that we belong to the mission and our very identity is indelibly marked by it.*[77]

In marriage the love-covenant of the couple gives them a new identity where everything is now in relationship with one another. The same is true in the love-covenant of shepherding the people of God. It gives the ordained a new identity where everything is now in relationship with God and God's people. The mission of *shepherding the church* has two parts to it according to Cardinal Jorge Bergoglio, who addressed the Synod of Bishops in Rome in 2001: overseeing (or watching over) and keeping watch.

> Overseeing refers more to a concern for doctrine and habits (behavior), whereas keeping watch is more about making sure that there be salt and light in people's heart. Watching over speaks of being alert to imminent danger; keeping watch, on the other hand, speaks of patiently bearing the processes through which the Lord carries out the salvation of his people. To watch over, it is enough to be awake, sharp, quick. To keep watch

you need also to be meek, patient, and constant in proven charity. Overseeing and watching over suggest a certain degree of necessary control. Keeping watch, on the other hand, suggests hope, the hope of the merciful Father who keeps watch over the processes in the hearts of his children.[78]

The path to being called to ordained ministry winds its way through the fields of theology (moral, systematic, pastoral, spiritual), scripture, canon law, church history, liturgy, homiletics with prerequisite disciplines like philosophy and its history, psychology, sociology, world history, literature, and more. Accompanying the academic path, there is the path involving spiritual direction, psychological testing, and evaluation along the way. All of these act as resources for knowing the tradition, structure, and the history of the church's proclamation of the good news of the reign of God, as revealed in and by Jesus Christ.

Shepherding the church involves bringing those resources to form and inform ministry to the people of God in a loving and appropriate way. This is where "the rubber meets the road," and to understand this love-covenant shepherding of the church, it is important to understand the foundation and development of the ministry of Jesus. If the ministry of the ordained is to reflect the mission and proclamation of Christ, then the ordained are clearly called to *have that mind in them that is in Christ Jesus* as Paul says to the Philippians in chapter 2 verse 5.

Jesus was formed and informed by the richness of the Hebrew scriptures: the Torah, the Prophets, and the Writings or Wisdom literature. Walter Brueggemann[79] says that these three canons represent the ordinary and healthy development not only of the coming to human consciousness but also of the coming to spiritual consciousness of the Kingdom of God that Jesus had come to proclaim. For Jesus, the Kingdom of God was always the implied focus of everything he said and did—if not the explicit subject at a given time. For Jesus, there was and is nothing that falls outside the province of the reign of God. His ministry, formed and informed by the Torah, the Prophets, and the Wisdom of the scriptures, was to help people recognize the reality of God's unique presence in their lives.

In Matthew 5:17 we read that Jesus said, "Do not think that I have come to abolish the law or the prophets; I have come not to abolish but to fulfill." In this short statement, we have reference to the Torah, which gave the Israelites the Law, structure, and a sense of being a people chosen by God. Then there are the Prophets who—through a healthy self-criticism, reflection, and thinking—envisioned where this concept of being chosen would take them. Thirdly, there is Wisdom, which is the fulfillment of both. Wisdom literature reveals the need to be patient with the mystery and contradictions in life, and instructs that being inspired and led by the Spirit of God takes one into depths and heights beyond imagining.

Matthew chapter 5 demonstrates how Jesus teaches from these three dimensions in a coherent way. He actually begins with the third dimension (wisdom) when, in the Sermon on the Mount, Jesus proclaims where happiness and blessedness can be found. Then Jesus assumes the prophetic stance when, in a series of statements concerning the Law, he says, "You have heard that it was said...but I say to you..." Jesus is affirming that the movement of the Law and the prophetic dimensions is always toward the wisdom dimension, unless one chooses not to go beyond the Law and/or the prophetic.

One can show his or her love for God by obeying the Ten Commandments. And that is not easy. But what is harder is to love one's neighbor *as oneself*. Jesus moves the act of loving even further when in John 15:12 he says, "This is my commandment, that you love one another *as I have loved you.*" And then he follows that by adding, "No one has greater love than this, *to lay down one's life for one's friends.*" Jesus has invited his disciples into a whole new dimension of love and one that he is about to demonstrate on the cross. In no way did he abolish either the Law or the prophets. Rather, he became the fulfillment of both. And this is the Kingdom of God's love, which the people of God are called to proclaim and live, and the ordained are called to shepherd.

Called and sent to proclaim a ministering Gospel

The period of training and preparing for ordination is long and intense. Then the day comes. And just like after the wedding a new reality sets in for the married couple, so after the ordination a new reality begins for the ordained. The virtual reality of lecture halls and classrooms will be traded for the reality of parish, school, or other places where ministry is needed. Practicing homilies and talks before peers will give way to standing face-to-face with a gathering of God's people. It is an anxious time.

Such was the case for the apostles prior to their going forth. Luke tells us in the Book of Acts, chapter 1, that the disciples withdrew to the upper room and spent time in waiting and prayer. So often they were witness to the fact that Jesus would withdraw to pray and open himself to learning the will of God. Jesus promised that the same Spirit of God that empowered Jesus would empower them.

> *Then [Jesus] opened their minds to understand the scriptures, and he said to them, "Thus it is written, that the Messiah is to suffer and to rise from the dead on the third day, and that repentance and forgiveness of sins is to be proclaimed in his name to all nations, beginning from Jerusalem. You are witnesses of these things."*[80]

That is why each day priests must stand before God and be open to the action of the Holy Spirit in their lives in order to know the *mind of Jesus*. One of the *spiritual exercises* of St. Ignatius Loyola is to place oneself in a Gospel scene or parable as one of the characters. This can help make the scene or parable more personal and thus make one more *mindful*. The purpose is to bring this *mindfulness* into whatever one is planning, doing, suffering, or whatever. Then as Jesus does, the good news of the Gospel will be bestowed upon the world in abundance.

In Mark's Gospel (4:1–20, as well as in Matthew 13:1–13 and Luke 8:4–10), Jesus tells the parable of the sower and the seeds. He tells us that the seeds are the Word of God. The sower is either both very generous and optimistic or very careless with where the seeds end up. Some of them land on the path, some on rocky ground, some among thorns, and some on rich soil. But perhaps the message is that as Jesus, the Sower, gives every piece of ground the opportunity to accept and yield the good news, so too do those who proclaim the good news through the ages. The ordained are missioned to proclaim it and let it go because it is God who gives the growth.

Thomas Aquinas is admired for his talent in philosophy and theology. His writing is an enormous accomplishment, and for that he is called the Angelic Doctor of the Church. However it didn't begin that way. Many of the theologians in his time were suspicious of his work because he brought together Aristotle's thought and the Christian teachings. But using the example of the parable of the sower and the seeds, it seemed that he was able to discover the seeds of good news in the pathways, the rocky soil, and the thickets, as well as in the rich soil of Aristotle's philosophy. Thomas recovered the seeds and gave them the chance to grow in Christian thought.

This is the work of the ordained priest in every generation—namely, the openness to be led by the Spirit to discover and/or recover the seeds of good news along the diverse landscape of earthly existence and then to proclaim it. The seeds that are discovered and/or recovered are those that were planted by others. And seeds that are newly scattered will be tended and harvested by later sowers and gatherers.

Obstacles in proclamation ministry

The last thing on the minds of brides and grooms on their wedding day are the obstacles that lay ahead of them. They know there will be obstacles. So as they put away the special garments chosen for the wedding, they clothe themselves with the spiritual garments necessary for the marriage.

The same is necessary for those ordained. On the day of ordination, they are clothed with special vestments. These, also, must be replaced with the spiritual garments that will sustain them for ordained ministry. So often there can be things that get in the way and that can complicate this ministry. Luke tells us how the disciples themselves got in their own way. James and John were suggesting that they call down fire upon the village that did not welcome them. So, one of the spiritual vestments needed is that of openness. Those who proclaim the Word of God must take time on a regular basis to reflect on how much they are truly open to the movement of the Spirit as well as how much they try to control the Spirit along paths that are more comfortable for them.

And then there is the need to be vested in listening and watching. Using the image of seeds and their ability to yield a harvest, one can easily think about a good growing season and a not-so-good growing season. In Ohio the good growing season would be defined as March (a little iffy) through October, while in the other months, the land was thought to be dormant. But recently there are some people who are growing vegetables year round and taking them to market year round. These growers have listened and learned from what the soil, air, moisture, and sun environment have revealed to them. They maintain an environment of growth from seed to harvest with the help of large areas enclosed in plastic sheeting that can be opened and closed depending on the day and temperature. They even manage a large population of ground worms to fertilize the initial seedbeds. They work with what nature has taught them and what the earth has given them. They have taken a landscape that is frozen and dormant and found a way to work toward a harvest. It's an effort that requires listening and watching skills, bonded in patience and trust. And both they and the land are richer for it. So it is with listening and watching the people of God.

Also needed is the vestment of courage. The work of proclamation of the Word requires effort. Jesus has entrusted the Gospel proclamation to the likes of mortals. What a responsibility, and, at the same time, what a privilege! When overwhelmed by it all because of a sense of inadequacy or fear of failure, priests must remind themselves that if they really get into living the Gospel, it will be proclaimed by their lives. They have to remind themselves that their preaching is by way of invitation. After all, like Jesus they are presenting an invitation to others that they can accept or not. This calls for the vestment of trust.

Proclaiming the good news of freedom

Then there is the vestment of integrity and faith. If the proclamation of the Gospel is not reflected in the lives of those who preach, then the preaching becomes shallow and a "noisy gong and clanging cymbal" (1 Corinthians 13:1).

The decisive orientation toward God in shepherding the church is a burden, but it is the burden of freedom—freedom to rely on God and flourish. Jesus does not make empty promises, and the lives of priests as proclaimers of the Gospel must be proof texts of that fact. As ordered members of the church, they must learn to order their lives to the Gospel of Christ before they can order the Body of Christ (the church).

In both the Gospels of Matthew and Luke, instructions on how the lives of Jesus's followers are to be ordered follows immediately after the call given to the disciples. In the Gospel of Matthew, Jesus teaches the beatitudes on the mountain, thus making the connection between Jesus and Moses, as the lawgiver on Sinai. For some reason the Ten Commandments seem to be preferred to the beatitudes by many christians The beatitudes should not be left as something mysterious and impossible to comprehend and do. Like life itself the only way the beatitudes can be appreciated is for them to be experienced and lived. They are Jesus's rule of life.

General Omar Bradley, in his 1948 Memorial Day address, said, "The world has achieved brilliance without wisdom, power without conscience. We have grasped the mystery of the atom and rejected the Sermon on the Mount. Ours is a world of nuclear giants and ethical midgets. We know more about war than we do about peace; more about killing than we do about living."[81]

Luke writes of Jesus coming down from the mountain and teaching on the plain and being at eye level among people. What Jesus chooses to address are the tough and difficult concerns of daily existence: poverty, hunger, grief, hatred, or being an outcast. Jesus does not address these concerns as social issues but as issues pointing to the future. Jesus is not insinuating that poverty—with its squalor, starvation, lack of education, poor sanitation, lack of security, and rampant diseases—makes anyone happy.

Pope Francis in addressing the issue of poverty says this: "Poverty as overcoming every kind of selfishness ...teaches us to trust in God's Providence. Poverty [is] a sign for the entire Church that it is not we who build the Kingdom of God...[rather] Christians in their poverty plant a seed so rich that it becomes a great tree, capable of filling the world with its fruit."[82]

Jesus is saying that if people are poor and do not learn detachment from the things and powers of the earth, and if they do not place their reliance upon God while being poor, then becoming prosperous will not benefit them much in the long run. If they cannot find God in their grief and when ostracized, it's unlikely they will acknowledge God in their laughter and when others speak well of them.

The other thing Jesus is saying is that people are not blessed simply because they are poor, grieving, hungry, or marginalized, just as they are not cursed because they are rich, well fed, laughing, and respected. People are blessed or cursed depending on whether or not they recognize their dependence on God, gratefully acknowledge God's gifts, and place their hope in God's promise. Therein lies true happiness. God loves people no matter their status. It is in the recognition that they are loved by their Creator that frees them to face their poverty, their grief, their hunger, and their being slandered, and thus they are able to rise above all of that.

Proclaiming the good news of happiness

The vestment of happiness can be surprisingly uncomfortable because it is difficult to figure out how to wear it. Anthony de Mello in a retreat to university students touches on this issue of happiness. He says, "The world is full of sorrow. The root of sorrow is attachment. The uprooting of sorrow is the dropping of attachment." Then he goes on to explain that attachment is the false belief that something causes one's happiness. If something/someone causes happiness and a person loses that something/someone, then the person's happiness is gone.

What an interesting human reaction it is that as soon as humans get what they desire, their first reaction is exhilaration, but their very next reaction—sometimes conscious, sometimes not so conscious—is fear: fear of losing what they have just gained. All the work and effort in acquiring something turns into a fear of losing it. Why? Because, they believe she, he, or it is the cause of their happiness.

The difference between imperfect love and the love of Jesus is that imperfect love wants to possess, to control, and to change the other. Jesus loved the world, reality, and people; the change happened because of the love. Love cannot be conditioned to change. As followers of Christ, we are to be like Jesus. We are here to love the world into change, not change it before we love it.

And then, where did we ever get the idea that love had to be earned? We see something of this dynamic and coming to understanding in Peter and his encounter with Cornelius. "I begin to see how God shows no partiality."

As soon as happiness is tied to something or someone, it becomes a chain of bondage. This doesn't mean that people do not set goals and dream dreams. But deep down they need to know that their happiness does not depend on that someone or something. At birth the umbilical cord attaching them to their mother was severed. Why? The answer is, so that they could learn to develop and live in freedom. Many people go through life holding their umbilical cord in their hand and plugging it in to wherever they think happiness might be for them. People unfortunately equate thrills and kicks with happiness. They do not realize that they will begin to enjoy things and people when they aren't possessed by them and when they do not try to possess and control them.

The good news of paradox

This calls for the vestment of spiritual insight. The paradox that Jesus is teaching in the beatitudes is that happiness and poverty are not mutually exclusive—neither is happiness and persecution, suffering, nor even death. That is why it is the preeminent responsibility of those proclaiming members of the people of God to live the beatitudes so that the people of God to whom they are ordered can take them and the beatitudes seriously and thus come to experience and know the happiness that Jesus promised.

Happiness is a way of being that is unobstructed by attachments; it is the way God created us. The story in Genesis is a perfect illustration. Adam and Eve—perfectly happy until they were convinced that they lacked something—chose to pursue the fruit from the tree of knowledge of good and evil. Only then did they realize they were naked. When they chose to no longer see the world and themselves through the eyes of

God but through their own eyes, they saw themselves diminished. So what do they do? They began the great cover-up: "…and they sewed fig leaves together and made loincloths for themselves" (Genesis 3:7). "Then they hid themselves from the presence of the Lord" (Genesis 3:8). They did not know what to do with their new knowledge. They tried to avoid God. They now became attached to their shame and guilt; their happiness had become obstructed. The world was now a place of labor—both in giving birth and in living. This original sin, this great desire for power, was then taught and passed on generation after generation.

The paradox of freedom and power

Freedom is a great gift. It does not mean that we are free to do anything we want. Rather it means that we are free to do what needs to be done. Getting that wrong leads to anarchy and social disaster. The banner of freedom is often waved over personal agendas instead of the common good.

On university campuses the byword is *academic freedom*. "Freedom" might be the vision and buzzword on campuses, but in many ways it is not the reality. Certain topics are not permitted in some lecture halls. Issues of religious belief among some psychologists and counselors are summarily dismissed as unimportant or irrelevant. Then there are power issues within certain departments and how the financial resources are allocated, among other issues. It can be paralyzing. And people get seriously hurt in this struggle.

Then, too, we see that in the church where "love and reconciliation" are bywords, *power* is also often the reality—from top to bottom or from inside out (to use Vatican II imagery). This, too, is so distracting and destructive—like the disciples arguing about who is the greatest among them, right after Jesus tells them he is going to Jerusalem to suffer and to die. And the scandal of the cross isn't so much that Jesus died but that he was delivered up by the religious authorities acting, they thought, in the name of God. Here is where the vestment for discerning power and powerlessness is critical.

We live in a world in which power is the greatest and most valuable form of currency. People seek it, steal it, fight for it, and kill for it. The most heinous and desperate acts known to history come from the quest for power. And when one coats *power* with a layer or two of *religion*, it can become blinding and deadly. It can hardly be seen as a blessing.

Because earthly power is so frequently used for selfish purposes, it's hard to remember that power is an attribute, a gift, of God and, consequently, an intrinsic good. It was power that first ordered Creation, and it was power that brought life into being. The power of dominion was the first gift God bestowed on humanity in its infancy in Genesis 1:26–31. It was a gift to serve our needs and the needs of God's creatures. The world became quite a different place when power became the master and not the servant.

To know what a Christian must do to engage power appropriately, we look to Jesus as our guide. No one had the potential to wield more power than he did. "Yet Jesus did not deem equality with God something to be clung to" (Philippians 2:6). Jesus chose to lay the power aside for his friends and for his enemies—in service to the needs of the whole world— simply because there was such a need, and he was the only one with the power to meet it. It is to this "service to the world" that the ordained are ordered. That was and is the plan of Jesus. He has no other plan.

In an age when we use terms like "shock and awe" to describe the activity of military might, it's hard to look up at a crucifix and recognize that this is heaven's most powerful weapon against evil. The cross is "shock and awe" in cosmic proportions. Love is affixed to wood and held up for the mockery of fools. The full force of human hatred is hurled in the direction of divine compassion. Jesus emptied himself of ultimate power so that it could serve the greatest good, now and forever. He forgave. And twenty centuries later, people still look upon the cross without understanding its implications. It is time for the vestment of forgiveness.

In a quiet and private place, Jesus imparts the same power to his friends. As we hear in the Gospel on Pentecost, he breathes his Spirit on them and gives them the ultimate authority: to forgive sins.

If the church has a treasure, it's not in a bank or in the beauty of its artwork, its landholdings, or the height of its global profile. The great wealth of the church is that it has been entrusted with the authority to reconcile the sinner. Imagine: The worst thing of which a human being is capable can be washed clean by a word. Evil can be transfigured by grace. The sinner can become the saint.

Jesus died on the cross for the forgiveness of sins. If forgiveness is the message, there should not be judgment in the minds and speech of his followers. Forgiveness is the greatest gift we can bestow on each other. No one can give it for us. It is the seedbed for growing peace and our only path to freedom. Jesus knew that when he forgave—not from a place of safety, but from the cross of suffering.

Forgiveness is not amnesty, not a pardon or a dropping of all charges because of a technicality. Nor does it mean that God is soft on crime or indifferent to the demands of justice. Yet it speaks volumes—in the clear tones of the language of Pentecost—that God uses absolute power to obtain not absolute judgment, but absolute mercy for sinners.

"Receive the Holy Spirit," Jesus said to the disciples, and such is also his challenge to his followers. How do we receive the Spirit? How do we let it renew lives? How do we let it lead to forgiveness? How can we be inspired not only to use our gifts but also to use them for the good of all? Finally, how can we accept the Spirit's strengthening of priestly and diaconal witness by a willingness to forgive?

In the Gospel of Luke, John the Baptist said, "I baptize you with water; but one who is more powerful than I is coming...He will baptize you with the Holy Spirit and fire" (Luke 3:16). At Pentecost, Jesus made good on John's words. Christ calls his disciples to take up the fruits of his Spirit today, and embrace his way of shepherding.

Being an ordained or ordered minister is not just the result of having episcopal hands placed on one's head, while the prayer of consecration is said. It is also really trying very hard to live the part, to become *the bread that is broken and the cup that is shared.* Priests are called and ordained not just to *do* Eucharist, but also to *be* Eucharist. We have to make sure that we proclaim Christ's presence in all the places that Christ chooses to be present. And he chooses to be present in the "bread that is broken and the cup that is shared." He is present and reserved in our tabernacles. He also chooses to be present in those who receive him. And he is present in "the least of my brothers and sisters." Embracing the mystery of the Incarnation and Transubstantiation is to grow into an understanding of Paul's statement that "we are the Body of Christ."

The Gospel ministers to those who proclaim it

As priests, whether by reason of our baptism or orders, if we really believe and live the Gospel message, we will see how it ministers to those as they proclaim it; how the Gospel both challenges and empowers us to be faithful; how the Gospel message dispels our fears and calls us to trust without reservation; how *forgiving* is the keystone to Jesus's message; how the Gospel is a message of life even in a culture of death; and, finally, how the Gospel helps us toward a decision of commitment. We will catch real glimpses of God's Kingdom and know God's people because we trust Jesus's Word. We will see how our lives have a direction because we will let go of the controls.

± Bringing the Rite to Life ±

The Eucharist calls and sends

To minister to, or shepherd, the people of God in a loving way, the priest must have some clue as to what makes for a loving way. For that to happen, the priest must come to understand the situations from whence the people come. Here is a simple example. The priest is very much aware of all the things that need to be done to get ready for a Sunday Mass. There are things like the bulletin, the prepared homily, perhaps helping to select music, making sure the necessary things are set out for Mass—or at least having someone do that, making sure there are enough extraordinary ministers of the Eucharist, lectors, servers, and lastly, being on time and focused.

So what is the attitude of the presider when, looking out over the people after the entrance procession, more people are still coming in, looking for a place to sit, and ushering their children into a pew? There is the temptation to be upset and put off, thinking, "Why don't they start getting ready earlier? Where's their respect for Mass?" Spending a Sunday morning watching my sister and brother-in-law trying to get themselves and the children ready for Mass cured me of any attitude other than marveling at their weekly perseverance. And that is just one example. "Having the mind of Jesus" opens us to accept latecomers and even early leavers—whatever their reasons.

Jesus said that "Sabbath was for the people" and not the other way around. The same is true of our shepherding ministry. Our ministry is for the people. Of course the temptation is strong to wonder, "Why don't they appreciate it?" But Jesus gave us the simple solution to keep us free from loading ourselves with hurt feelings or the desire to call down fire and brimstone. He told us, for the time being, just to shake the dust off and move on. Keeping score isn't part of the ministry. In shepherding God's people, like in shepherding children, things can go from the sublime to the ridiculous and back again in very short order. We see that happen when Jesus was trying to prepare the disciples for his coming passion and suffering and they were arguing about who among them was the greatest. After that, nothing people do should be a surprise.

The Good Shepherd

In the Gospel of John, Jesus speaks to quality shepherding.[83] According to Jesus's criteria, there seem to be two parts to this quality of shepherding: one is that the sheep follow him because they recognize his voice; the second is that they recognize his voice as he calls his own sheep by name. Quality shepherding isn't about knowing individual people by name. Jesus certainly did not know all of the names of those in the crowds that followed him. They followed him because they realized from his teaching that he understood them and their hopes and needs. He was able to identify with their situations and speak to those situations. And that is the task of those ordained to shepherd, namely, to understand the hopes and needs of the people and proclaim the Gospel out of that understanding. That means being open to learning about the dynamics of the environment, culture, and setting of the folks to whom the Gospel is addressed. Jesus's words could vary from being words of comfort, encouragement, praise, challenge, and even rebuke. But they were words always spoken with love and care. The message Jesus proclaimed was not always welcomed or accepted. But it was always on target and, to a great degree, understood.

The universal dynamic of Eucharist

Pierre Teilhard de Chardin, SJ, was professor of geology at the Catholic Institute in Paris, director of the National Geologic Survey of China, and director of the National Research Center of France. He died in New York City in 1955. He worked hard both as a theologian and as a scientist. He saw that both theology and science were open ended. New findings led to more questions, which made for new possibilities. He firmly believed that all creation had its beginning in God and was moving toward a common destiny, which was God. If there is such a thing as truth (and there is) then there can be no conflict in theology or science, only in the theologian and the scientist because of the limits they embrace.

Here is his reflection on "The Mass on the World."[84]

Since once again, Lord—though this time not in the forests of the Aisne but in the steppes of Asia—I have neither bread, nor wine, nor altar, I will raise myself beyond these symbols, up to the pure majesty of the Real itself; I, your priest, will make the whole earth my altar and on it will offer you all the labors and sufferings of the world.
Over there, on the horizon, the sun has just touched with light the outermost fringe of the

eastern sky. Once again, beneath this moving sheet of fire, the living surface of the earth wakes and trembles, and once again begins its fearful travail. I will place on my paten, O God, the harvest to be won by this renewal of labor. Into my chalice I shall pour all the sap which is to be pressed out this day from the earth's fruits.

My paten and my chalice are the depths of a soul laid widely open to all the forces which in a moment will rise up from every corner of the earth and converge upon the Spirit. Grant me the remembrance and the mystic presence of all those whom the light is now awakening to the new day…

Over every living thing which is to spring up, to grow, to flower, to ripen during this day say again the words: "This is my Body." And over every death-force which waits in readiness to corrode, to wither, to cut down, speak again your commanding words which express the supreme mystery of faith: "This is my Blood."

Much study, research, and writing is focused on the scriptural basis for the liturgy of the Eucharist—the rubrics or the correct and accepted way to celebrate Mass and who qualifies and is ordered to preside. Obviously, these elements are necessary. But there is more, and it is this: where does our celebration take us as God's people? It can't stop at the altar or the tabernacle or the Sacred Elements or the people gathered around the altar. To do so would be to make of all these important parts of the celebration simply "mute idols."

It took the disciples some time to come to an understanding of what Jesus was doing when he broke the bread and passed the chalice saying, "This is my body; this is the cup of my blood. Do this in memory of me." The simple act of breaking bread and sharing a cup of wine in memory of Jesus would not have taken them very far in the face of their own mission and persecution unless they came to an understanding of where and to whom this action and remembering was leading them. They came to understand that whenever they went to Jesus, he proclaimed, announced, and pointed to the reign of God. Jesus did not let them get comfortable in the upper room for long. With the signs of wind and flame, he urged them to go out among the people where they would see the reign of God so that they could proclaim it. The reign of God cannot be proclaimed in a closed vacuum. That is the reason why the proclamation at the end of Mass is not "we are done here; you can go home now." Rather it is "go, announce the Gospel of the Lord" or "go in peace, glorifying the Lord by your life." That work is ongoing.

The rite of the Sacrament of Holy Orders has a place and time. Let us pray that the fruit of the sacrament becomes an integral part of our life now and forever.

Conclusion

The church and science

There seems to be a ready acceptance that technology and faith—science and religion—are mutually exclusive, always at odds with each other, or, at best, uneasy partners. The examples generally used are that of Galileo, Copernicus, or Pierre Teilhard de Chardin. The reactions by some ecclesiastical officials in these cases have haunted the church through the years.

But those who know the history of science know that many of the most accomplished scientists in history were associated with the Church. There is the Jesuit, Athanasius Kircher, who said, "Nothing in God's world should escape our notice and our wonder." Besides being very learned in ancient and Oriental languages, he was a student of medicine, philosophy, mathematics, optics, and geology. Then there is Father Roger Bacon (the medieval chemist), Father Gregor Mendel (the man whose humble botanical work earned him the right to be called the father of genetics), Father George Lemaître (the astrophysicist to whom we owe the theory of the Big Bang).

Then there is Thomas Aquinas, the star pupil of Albert (called the Great because of his encyclopedic knowledge) who, like Kircher, was a biologist, collector and analyzer of plants and animals. Many theologians feared that too much emphasis on the world would blind us to the world beyond, but in their fear lurked the heretical deprecation of matter, and not the joyful wonder of Genesis. Aquinas, Kircher, Bacon, Mendel, Lemaître, Albert, and so many others helped to save the world for the faith, and the faith for the world.[85]

Through the years, especially in western cultures, there has been a general acceptance among people that faith is weaker than knowledge, that believing is second best to knowing, that all mysteries need to be solved to be relevant, and that spiritual things are suspect when not understandable and/or able to be scientifically proven.

Rabbi Jonathan Sacks, former chief rabbi of the United Kingdom, summarized the difference between science and religion in two sentences: "Science takes things apart to see how they work. Religion puts them together to see what they mean."[86]

In recent years the very science that we engage to give us the knowledge we desire has stumbled upon a rather unique mystery that is gaining acceptance and about which much theorizing is being developed. It has to do with *dark energy* and *dark matter*. (For more information see the NASA website.)[87]

Obviously, the mystery of the universe will fuel much debate and scientific research for years to come. What I find awesome about the points made in this article from the NASA website is that a close analogy can be made between the mystery of the universe and the mystery of the human person. Most people on planet earth are simply not aware of the mysteries of the material universe of which they are a part. Their vision is very limited—usually to what they see around themselves. The Hubble Space Telescope has opened for us a whole new way to see our universe. The images that it gives us are awesome and breathtaking. The number of not only planets but also galaxies is staggering. The Hubble Space Telescope has revealed so much to us that we simply could not see with our limited sight.

> More is unknown than is known. We know how much dark energy there is because we know how it affects the Universe's expansion. Other than that, it is a complete mystery. But it is an important mystery. It turns out that *roughly 68 percent* of the Universe is dark energy. Dark matter makes up about 27 percent. The rest—everything on Earth, everything ever observed with all of our instruments, all normal matter—adds up to less than 5 percent of the Universe. Come to think of it, maybe it shouldn't be called "normal" matter at all, since it is such a small fraction of the Universe.[88]

Much the same can be said about the human person. *More is unknown than is known.* Much of what we know about people is how they affect our senses. *Other than that, they are a complete mystery.* Ninety-five percent of the universe is dark—dark energy and dark matter. The same can be said about ourselves. There is such a width and depth to every person—a width and depth that continue to expand. We know that the 5 percent *normal matter* has it limits. So it is with the *normal matter* of the person. But it is the *dark energy and dark matter* that expand. In the human person, for the sake of analogy and leaving the percentages aside, I would like to think of that mysterious energy as *faith* and that mysterious matter as *the human spirit or soul.* In fact, our physical and material self is a small fraction of who we are. Yet, so much of our time, money, and effort is bound up in that small fraction.

Part of the reason we get all tied up with that small fraction of ourselves is that we do not understand or appreciate the *spirit side* of who we are. How much time do people spend with the *spirit side* of their being, trying to comprehend the complexity and dimensions of all that they are and, more importantly, of all that they can be.

> One explanation for dark energy is that it is a property of space. Albert Einstein was the first person to realize that empty space is not nothing. Space has amazing properties, many of which are just beginning to be understood. The first property that Einstein discovered is that it is possible for more space to come into existence.[89]

Like Einstein realized about space, namely *that empty space is not nothing,* we have to realize that our *spirit side is not nothing.* Our *spirit side* has *amazing properties,* and we have hardly even begun to understand those properties because we have spent so much time with the physical and material, which we find slowly deteriorates. On the other hand, our *spirit side* expands and creates more space.

> Then one version of Einstein's gravity theory, the version that contains a *cosmological constant,* makes a second prediction: "empty space" can possess its own energy. Because this energy is a property of space itself, it would not be diluted as space expands. As more space comes into existence, more of this energy-of-space would appear. As a result, this form of energy would cause the Universe to expand faster and faster. Unfortunately, no one understands why the cosmological constant should even be there, much less why it would have exactly the right value to cause the observed acceleration of the Universe.[90]

For the sake of my analogy, I would like to call this *cosmological constant,* "faith." This faith is a constant that possesses its own energy, an energy that will not be diluted as one's life expands. It is with this energy of faith that we can choose to believe and come to some comprehension of the immense and tremendous image and likeness of God, of which we and all creation have been gifted.

The light of faith and the life of the sacraments

That was the message that Christ revealed to us in so many ways, images, and parables. Like the Hubble Space Telescope, Jesus presented us with remarkable and awesome views of our spiritual universe: the Kingdom of God. Like most people who are not aware of the mysteries of our material universe, so people are not aware of the mysteries of our spiritual universe. Christ is all about revealing this universe of the spirit. The Kingdom of God is like leaven, a person in search of fine pearls, a tiny mustard seed, a woman who found her lost coin, a king who gives a banquet, a man who sows seeds, a father who divides his inheritance between his two sons, and on and on. These images and parables seem so simple at first glance, but they are powerful and deep in their application and meaning. As we unwrap them, and if we let them, they take us to a point of self-revelation and God revelation. It is Teilhard's Omega Point for all creation. Just like we are part of this great mystery we call our universe, we are part of this great mystery we come to know as Creator.

God has given us many remarkable gifts—both material and spiritual. Our ability to trust enough so that we can come to believe and to believe enough so that we can come to experience, know, and grow is awesome. It is essential for both our material well-being and our spiritual well-being. This God-given ability helps us to find meaning in our life even in the face of difficulties and suffering. It sustains us in patient waiting as our life unfolds. It gives our spirit buoyancy even as waves of fear, despair, and darkness try to overwhelm us. It gives us confidence that our life, far from being narrow and closed ended, is ever widening and opening endlessly into eternity.

For us to see this, we must resist the temptation to see faith only as *creed* and sacraments only as *rituals*. Rather, they are thresholds and models for living in the Kingdom of God—now and at every moment of our life on earth. That is what Jesus meant when he said that the Kingdom of God is already in our midst, not only in big things but also in little things that—by the power of God—can grow into big things. Our faith can grow to the point where it influences every moment of our lives because we have allowed ourselves to recognize that God has woven it into the very fabric of our being.

The sacraments empower the living of our lives, beginning in ritual but growing into who we are and can become. As we are recognized and named at birth, we carry that identity through life as "Thomas" or "Theresa." So at baptism we are recognized and named as a child of God, thus given an identity that we will carry throughout our earthly life into eternity. Confirmation seals our being ensouled by the Holy Spirit. Eucharist gathers us and nourishes us as the people of God. Marriage seals the love-covenant of the couple shepherding the home and exemplifying the love-covenant of God. Holy Orders seals the love-covenant of the ordained shepherding the church and exemplifying the shepherding love of God. Reconciliation and the Sacrament of Anointing of the Sick sustain and move us through an imperfect world toward a restoration of original innocence in our spirit and a body made whole by our resurrection.

We live and move and have our being not only in an amazing universe, but we also live and move and have our being in an amazing God. And it is our faith that can power and empower our living and moving and being in the *light* energy and matter of God's love.

Having that mind which was in Christ Jesus

Trying to maintain some degree of equilibrium and meaning in the midst of life's many mysteries can be an overwhelming task. Trying to develop a way for doing it can even be more confusing. As we come to the recognition that we have this *awesome ability to believe*, our next step is to decide *what to believe* that will give meaning to our life. For those who choose the way of Jesus, it behooves us to follow the advice that Paul gives to the Philippians in chapter 2, verse 5, "Let the same mind be in you that was in Christ Jesus." Our faith gives us the ability to do that, and the sacraments are signs and aids to sustain us in this endeavor.

The teachings and ministry of Jesus, flowing out of the Hebrew scriptures and tradition, must be our source for acquiring the mind of Christ Jesus in our life. What follows is an attempt in a very limited way to consider the mind of Jesus in a few specific examples from his teaching and ministry.

The temptation set before Adam and Eve in the garden was in regard to attaining power so as to be like God. Eating the fruit of the tree of knowledge of good and evil was the way of acquiring that likeness, so claimed the tempter. What resulted was, however, quite different. In place of power, they found themselves naked, fragile, and overcome by fear and shame.

The temptation set before Jesus in the desert was also in regard to attaining power. Turning stone into bread would satisfy hunger and give life, so claimed the tempter. Jesus's response was, "One does not live by bread alone, but by every word that comes from the mouth of God" (Matthew 4:4). What resulted was a comfortableness with limitations and the path to acquiring and maintaining our likeness to God.

Father Alfred Delp, SJ,[91] was one of the millions of victims of Nazi paranoia in search of power. He said that humanity has permanent need of supernatural power and strength. Power is good and is a gift from God. The problem arises when our communication with the divine is stopped. Then we begin to have strange dreams and set up the false gods of success, power by force, and a new order of the world. But we do not get very far because "we keep running up against our own limitations and the insufficiency of our creative efforts." This is a repeat of the story of the garden, and, unfortunately, it seems to have been the default solution through much of human history.

In the story of Jesus in the desert, we get a clear insight into the mind of Jesus. Communication with the divine is maintained and is always a priority. One needs bread to live, yes. But one also needs to be nourished by every word of God. Trying to listen to God's Word might seem like a difficult—if not downright mysterious—task. But basically God utters only one eternal word: love. From that word came forth creation and all that is good. And then "the Word became flesh and dwelt among us." The personal sign of God's love is Jesus, the Anointed One. Jesus said many things—all of which attempt to give us a glimpse of God's love for us.

Jesus came announcing the reign of God, which is the environment where humanity is in a state of grace, where human needs are met by God's abundance, human limitations are resolved by God's power, and human rashness is forgiven and tamed by God's discipline. In this order of God, the personal pronoun "I" gives way to "we." The prayer Jesus taught is evidence of this: *Our* Father, *our* daily bread, and forgive *us our* trespasses as *we* forgive those who trespass against *us*. The life of faith is never just "God and me." Jesus tries to teach us that we are all connected.

Jesus maintains the significance of *we* very clearly in the parable of the last judgment in Matthew 25, where the criteria for entry into eternal life is not a test of knowledge but of deeds easily doable out of love for others. It means that we have to watch out for one another. This in no way lessens our dignity or our place in the reign of God as individuals; it only requires that we be aware of our responsibility in the family of God. It's when we disconnect ourselves from the common task of caring that we are at risk of losing our *self*.

Jesus seems to be of the mind that people who are poor in spirit—who mourn, are meek, hunger and thirst for righteousness, are merciful, clean of heart, peacemakers, and persecuted—are blessed…or at least can be. And if they live out that blessedness, they become salt of the earth and the light of the nations. (See Matthew 5:3–13.) Jesus is of the mind that if we go to the root cause of many of our problems, we can deal with them before they become a major issue in our lives. He is not about abolishing the law and prophets but rather fulfilling them by making them meaningful. (See Matthew 5:17.) Jesus also sees that feeding anger or allowing one's imagination to reduce others to mere objects of one's own selfishness leads to all kinds of problems. (See Matt. 5:21, 27.)

Refusing to forgive can also become a very heavy burden. So Jesus tells us to lighten the load by forgiving others, even enemies. Some people are reluctant to forgive because that might seem like they are letting the culprits get away with something. Forgiveness is not complicity with whatever the wrong was. Refusing to forgive binds us more closely to the wrong over time.

Jesus is also of the mind that our words and deeds are trustworthy when we are trustworthy. We should do things not for show but because there are things that should be done, and we should be sincere in doing them. Nor should we waste time worrying, living in fear, or judging. Those things tend to paralyze our spirit. When we are overwhelmed and burdened by life, we should turn to him and find rest.

Jesus is always about doing the will of God. Complicated? If the word of God comes out of the will of God, then it is all about love. It is that simple. So what is the problem? Jesus knows that the love of God is unconditional and without limit. So the problem isn't really God—nor does it have to be us, provided we make every effort to intentionally try to love unconditionally and without limiting our love. That is what Jesus did, and the more we try, the more we will have that mind which was in Christ Jesus. Now wouldn't that be awesome?

All...were by nature foolish who were in ignorance of God, and who from the good things seen did not succeed in knowing the One who is, and from studying the works did not discern the artisan...For if they so far succeeded in knowledge that they could speculate about the world, how did they not more quickly find its Lord? (Wisdom 13:1-2,9)

Dying is not the worst tragedy that can happen to us. Living without faith is a far greater tragedy.

Appendix

Points for reflection and/or discussion

Understanding my ability to believe

Can I recall a time when God answered my prayer? What feelings does that memory stir up in me?

Can I recall a time when I think God substituted something I needed but did not ask for? What feelings does that memory stir up in me?

In what specific ways does my ability to believe affect the manner in which I engage life? In what ways do I see God's Kingdom unfolding in my life?

Can I recall a "mustard-seed" experience? Does it continue to grow in me?

Do I regularly take time in my motion-picture living to reflect on events in a still-life manner in order to enjoy the quality and richness of those moments?

Do I better comprehend the understanding that my ability to believe is the dynamic way I relate not only to God but also to God's creation, in general, and to God's people in particular?

Can I recall a situation when my ability to believe has opened up for me a whole new way to view reality? What was that like for me?

Does my experience affirm that love requires faith and that in expressing love my faith and trust grow?

Do I believe that God accompanies me on my life's journey? Am I comfortable with the idea of walking with God and God walking with me in the garden of my life?

How comfortable am I with the thought that the Spirit of God dwells in my heart?

Do I have a fear of God because I am in dread of God or because I am in awe of God?

In what ways do I make the parables of Jesus personal?

Understanding my baptismal identity

Do I recall a time in my life when I intentionally accepted the members of my human family as my family? If yes, what was the reason? If not sure, how do I feel about taking a moment now to do it—one member at a time?

Have I consciously considered my place in my human family? Given the fact that all families encounter rough patches at times, have I reflected on the ways I have been affirmed and enriched?

Am I clear about my responsibilities toward the members of my family? How have these responsibilities developed through time?

What are the ways that I keep myself from taking my family for granted?

What long-term gifts has my family brought into my life? What long-term gifts do I think I have brought into my family?

How would I describe the spirit of my family?

When I think about my identity—who I am—does it occur to me that I am a beloved child of God?

Have I consciously considered my place in my family of faith? Have I taken the time to reflect on the ways my faith family has affirmed and enriched my life?

What for me really defines my identity? How satisfactory are my responses to that question?

Have I ever given any thought to what being born into my human life means to me?

Have I ever given any thought to what being "born again" in baptism means to me?

Have I ever considered where the reality of me starts and stops? How do I live with the mystery of not really knowing the answer to that question?

How believable is it for me that I am a child of God, loved without any condition?

Baptism is a faith sign that I am loved by God not because of what I do or don't do but simply because I exist. Am I trying to grow into that understanding?

Do I understand that the basis for all the good news that Jesus revealed is the reality of God's love for me?

Am I able to offset and balance the bad news in my life with the good news?

Do I understand that the grace of baptism is a grace for the whole of life—human and divine?

What are some of the ways that I use to remind me of my baptism?

When I notice the names of the newly baptized in the parish bulletin, do I offer a silent prayer of welcome to them into the family of God?

Understanding my confirmation call

How would I describe the spirit of my family? Do I enjoy family time: meals, trips together, visiting relatives, family reunions? How do I show my appreciation?

How conscious am I of my faith family—the people with whom I worship on a regular basis?

Am I becoming more conscious of other groupings of family besides my own?

Is belonging to the family of God becoming more real for me? What are some of the things that help to make it more real?

Is the belief that I am a child of God, created in love, being confirmed in me?

Am I becoming more aware of what it means to have faith in God and in Jesus?

Am I more open to believing that the Spirit of God works through my faith family, helping me to come to a deeper faith about the love of God?

Can I recall a time when I felt that I had to stand up with and for my family or for some members of my family or for my family values?

Are there times when I feel the need to stand up with and for my faith family by witnessing to the values we hold and respect?

Do I understand that the Sacrament of Confirmation celebrates my call to grow into a disciple of Jesus by listening to the good news of the Gospel and proclaiming it by the way I live? Do I understand that it is a lifelong process of listening and proclaiming?

Am I growing into an understanding of the spirit side of who I am?

Am I growing in my trust of God?

Am I growing in my trust of life?

Am I growing in my trust that my life has a purpose—an eternal purpose?

How do I come to appreciate my gifts and talents? What do I do to help them become stronger?

How do I come to recognize and appreciate the gifts of the Spirit: wisdom, understanding, right judgment, courage, knowledge, reverence, wonder, and awe?

How has the spirit of wisdom and understanding grown in the way I think? How has the spirit of right judgment and courage grown in the way I search for truth? How has the spirit of knowledge and reverence grown in the way I view the universe? How has the spirit of wonder and awe grown in the way I embrace my life?

How do I understand Jesus saying that he is "the way and the truth and the life"?
What questions do I most often bring to God in prayer? Do I trust God with my doubts?

Have I come to appreciate and trust my human family? What are some of the gifts I have received from my personal family?

Have I come to appreciate my faith family? What are some of the gifts that I have received from them?

Where in my life have I experienced the fruits of the Spirit of God: love, joy, and peace; doing things with greater patience, kindness, and goodness; growing more comfortable with long-suffering, meekness, and faith; and reflecting in my thoughts and behavior moderation, modesty, and chastity?

In what ways have the works of mercy become more natural for me?

Understanding my Eucharistic call

Was making or receiving my First Communion a significant event for me? Why? Why not?

Is making or receiving my umpteenth Communion a significant event for me? Why? Why not?

What are some of the ways I have incorporated Eucharist into my daily living? Have I been able to bring my daily living as an offering to Eucharist?

In what ways have I been able to show respect to my belief in the real presence in the tabernacle? Do I understand that when I receive Eucharist I become a living tabernacle? Do I understand that when the person next to me receives Eucharist he or she becomes a living tabernacle?

In what ways for me has Eucharist become a significant context for daily living?
When I am with others, how do I share my presence? How do I experience their presence?

Have I come to understand the Eucharistic overtones of the last judgment scene from Matthew's Gospel: "Whatever you do to the least of my brothers and sisters you do to me?"

As I understand that all the members of my physical body, although diverse, must work together for the good of the whole body, how do I express that understanding when it comes to the Body of Christ—the people of God?

Is it easier for me to identify the things that divide people or the things that tend to unite them?

What are some items that I keep and treasure in memory of someone or some event? Why is this important to me? Does it function as a *point of union* with that something or someone?

When our bodies are not nourished in a timely fashion, they send out hunger signals. How easy is it for me to identify and respond to the hunger signals of my spirit?

Have I made the connection between the dinner table at home around which family and friends gather, the Eucharistic table in my church around which are gathered the people of God and the Eucharistic banquet table in the Kingdom of God around which are gathered the communion of saints?

Am I growing into a greater awareness of the various ways that the mystery of the Eucharist challenges me?

Understanding the healing grace of reconciling my sinfulness

In what ways have I grown into a better understanding of why Jesus asks me to leave my gift at the altar, go be reconciled with others, and then come offer my gift?

In what ways have I come to an understanding that sin is more about fracturing relationships than breaking laws?

In what ways have I come to understand that reconciliation is about healing relationships?

For me, is the journey to reconciliation driven by guilt and/or shame or by a deeper desire to be at one with another?

Does remembering that I am a person in whom the Spirit of God dwells influence how I think and act?

Do I understand that I am more prone to sin when I forget that I am made in the image and likeness of God?

Do I understand the many ways that I am my "brothers' [and sisters'] keeper"?

Do I understand that the first step to reconciliation is about *coming to myself, coming to my senses*, and *coming to understand who I am*?

Do I understand that my first response to forgiveness should be gratefulness to God?

Do I understand that my second response to forgiveness is a willingness to extend that forgiveness to others?

Do I understand that the greatest danger of feeling self-righteous is the inability to recognize my sin and thus the inability to appreciate forgiveness?

Am I comfortable with knowing that I live and move and have my being in the environment of God's forgiveness and not my worthiness?

Thomas Merton[92] said, "God is asking me, the unworthy, to forget my worthiness…and dare to advance in the love which has redeemed and renewed us all in God's likeness. And to laugh…at the preposterous idea of [our] worthiness. " How does Merton's statement strike me?

At what point have I come to understand that sin has never delivered, in the long run, on any of its promises?

When I examine my conscience, do I include the good things that I try to do?

Do I understand that, after opening myself to God's forgiveness, I must let go of my sin and the guilt and shame that accompany it and turn my attention to doing the good I am capable, with God's grace, of doing?

I take aspirin for headaches and use bandages for cuts and bruises. What do I do about a bad attitude or bruising words?

Do I understand that to be created in the image and likeness of God is to make forgiveness a major part of my identity?

At what point have I come to understand better the sources of the healing power of reconciliation? In what ways am I growing into a person of honor, respect, and integrity?

Understanding the healing grace of anointing my mortality

What is my understanding of the Sacrament of the Anointing of the Sick?

In what ways am I growing in my courage to confront the reality of my being mortal? Am I able to act on the truth that I find?

The Sacrament of Confirmation was able to help me recognize the gifts of the Holy Spirit in my life. Am I more apt to pray for the gifts of wisdom, understanding, and courage as I am being confronted by the mystery and complexity of living?

How am I trying to maintain a healthy lifestyle for both my body and my spirit?

In what ways do I consider myself a caregiver?

Am I becoming more aware of the various difficulties that the sick and disabled must face?

How comfortable am I around people who are weakened because of illness or age?

Do I make a point of visiting the sick or those confined to their homes or a care center? Or do I avoid doing that? Do I dare ask myself why I avoid visiting them?

How much do I know about hospice care? Is that something about which I should learn more?

Am I aware of some of the ways that those who are ill or disabled can witness to those who are healthy? How valuable do I think that witness is for me? How grateful am I for the level of health I presently have?

In what ways do I make myself aware of the dedication of health caregivers (like doctors, nurses, and EMTs)? How about those who help maintain the health of the community by collecting garbage and recyclables, those folks who maintain the water and sanitation services, and those who protect—like firefighters and police?

Am I aware of the healing power of conversation—or perhaps silence—or a smile or a simple sign of recognition or laughter and song? What else might I add to this list?

Understanding the grace of shepherding the home

When I think of the word "wedding," what comes to mind? When I think of the word "marriage," what comes to mind?

When I hear that "real intimacy comes only with vulnerability," what thoughts arise in me? How aware do I think most people are in realizing that real intimacy involves giving another the power to break their heart? Do I believe it? If I do, does that thought make me feel fearful, more committed, or a little of both?

Some think that Jesus used the symbol of the marriage covenant to best reflect God's covenant of love with the people. What is my reaction to that statement?

What, for me, are some of the most important qualities or building blocks for a healthy marriage?

Do I agree with the statement "a wedding is a most radical event"?

What do I think are some of the significant benefits of a wedding being celebrated in a communal setting? In a religious setting?

In what ways do I think that marriages model and minister quality love to society in general?

How do I think that our society in general helps or hurts marriages…families?

What do I think about the statement "sustaining love in marriage is not a matter of feelings but of decisions"?

What things help me to transition from a *me* focus to an *us* focus? How does this concept apply as a member of a team…as a member of a family…as a married couple?

Do I believe couples can grow richer and deeper in love through the years? What do I think would be some of the things necessary for this to happen?

Understanding the grace of shepherding the church

At Eucharist how aware am I of my priestly role by reason of my baptism?

Do I understand the purpose and ministry of the priestly role by reason of ordination?

If the love-covenant in service to the domestic church demands vulnerability, in what ways do I think the love-covenant in service to the liturgical church demands vulnerability?

When handed the book of the Gospels, the ordained priest hears these words: "Receive the book of the Gospels whose herald you are; believe what you read, teach what you believe, and practice what you teach." In what ways have I come to realize it is that truth which defines the ordained priest?

In what ways do I see the service of the ordained as a "laying down of one's life" for the family of God?

What would be some of the ways that I think the Gospels minister to those who proclaim the good news?

Like the disciples on the road to Emmaus, how have I experienced Jesus walking with me and opening the scriptures?

Jesus did not choose angelic beings but human beings to proclaim the Kingdom of God. Why do I think it is important that those ordained should be called from the community of the baptized?

How can I grow in the call to have that mind which is in Christ Jesus?

How can the ordained maintain a healthy tension and balance: between the call to ordained service and the call to a prophetic mission, between teaching and observing the letter of the law and its spirit, and between an institutional ministry that is faithful and a pastoral ministry that is mindful of the needs of people?

In the parable of the sower and the seeds, it seems that the sower is very generous in the scattering of the seeds. How can those ordained imitate this kind of generosity in the proclamation of God's Kingdom?

How can those who are ordained imitate the generous mercy given to both the younger and the elder son by the father in the parable of the prodigal?

How difficult do I think it is to maintain a degree of certainty about the kingdom of a God who seems to be a God so full of surprises?

What degree of risk and faith do I think it takes to preach the beatitudes?

What degree of risk and faith do I think it takes to live the beatitudes?

What are some of the difficulties in preaching detachment in a consumer society, freedom and happiness in a society immersed in power struggles, and social justice and the preferential option for the poor in an atmosphere of expediency? How did Jesus do it?

What do I think General Omar Bradley meant when he said, "Ours is a world of nuclear giants and ethical midgets?"

What do I think is the difference between "loving God above all things" and "loving all things in God and loving God in all things"?

How can those ordained witness to the unconditional love and mercy of God?

How can those ordained give witness to the fact that God uses absolute power to render not judgment, but mercy?

In what ways do I think that those ordained can not only *do Eucharist* but *become Eucharist*?

Conclusion

How surprising is it that some of the great scientists through history have been men and women of faith?

In the pursuit of knowledge, do I think my ability to believe is diminished? In my pursuit of faith, do I think my ability to know is diminished? Can they coexist?

Am I becoming more aware of the mystery of our universe— both its macroscopic and microscopic dimensions and the fact that more is unknown than known?

Am I becoming more aware of the mystery that I am? The mystery that each person is? The concept that more is unknown than known?

How comfortable am I living with these mysteries?

Our physical and material selves slowly deteriorate. Our spiritual selves expand and create space. How do I take advantage of this?

Christ is all about revealing the universe of the spirit. How do I take advantage of that?

Science knows how much dark energy there is because of how it affects the universe's expansion. Can I make a similar statement about the human spirit regarding its effect on my physical self?

Science is more certain what dark matter *is not* than what it *is*. Can I say the same about the human spirit? The soul?

Science and knowledge reveals to us that we live and move and have our being in an amazing universe. And Christ and faith in Christ reveal to us that we move and have our being in an amazing God. Doesn't it seem that both our physical and spiritual selves are well served?

Like Adam and Eve, why do we humans—made of both material and spiritual dimensions—keep putting the best of both at odds?

Notes, Permissions, and Credits

Prologue:

* Donna Leon, "The Golden Egg" 2013 Atlantic Monthly Press, New York. cit. page 35.

** Father Simon Tugwell O. P., "*Prayer: Living with God.* 1975 Templegate Publishers, 302 East Adams Street, Springfield, IL 62705-5152 www.templegate.com. Used with permission of the publisher.

Introduction:

[1] QED" represents the Latin phrase *quod erat demonstratum*: what was to be demonstrated. The phrase is traditionally placed in its abbreviated form at the end of a mathematical proof or philosophical argument.

[2] Michael Leach, "Soul Searching," *National Catholic Reporter*, vol. 50, no. 2 (2013): http://ncronline.org/blogs/soul-seeing/what-organ-sees-invisible (In this column Leach quotes the psychiatrist Dr. Thomas Hora. Used with permission of the publisher.)

[3] Richard Rohr's Daily Meditations," Richard Rohr, Center for Action and Contemplation, August 1, 2015, (Adapted from *A New Way of Seeing, a New Way of Being: Jesus and Paul.* Used with permission of the publisher.) cac.org PO Box 12464 Albuquerque, NM 87195

[4] Ibid.

[5] Ibid.

Chapter One: A Life Open to Believing

[6] Richard Rohr and John Bookser Feister, *Jesus' Plan for a New World,* St. Anthony Messenger Press, 1996 © Richard Rohr and John Bookser Feister, is reprinted with permission of the publisher cit. page vi .) cac.org PO Box 12464 Albuquerque, NM 87195

[7] *Man's Search for Meaning* by Viktor Frankl Copyright ©1959, 1962, 1984, 1992 by Viktor E. Frankl cit. page 100 Reprinted by permission of Beacon Press, ©2006 Beacon Press – Boston Massachusetts, 25 Beacon Street, Boston MA 02108-2892, www.beacon.org

[8] Ibid, cit. page 66.

[9] Ibid, cit. page 13.

[10] Ibid, cit. page 77.

[11] Ibid, cit. page 139–140.

[12] Ibid, cit. page 99.

[13] Ibid, cit. page x.

[14] Copyright ☐☐1952, 1953, 1981 by Alcoholics Anonymous Publishing (now known as Alcoholics Anonymous World Services, Inc.) All rights reserved. For all twelve steps go to: *cit. smf 121 -* .http://www.aa.org/assets/en_US/smf-121_en.pdf1

[15] *Man's Search for Meaning* by Viktor Frankl Copyright ©1959, 1962, 1984, 1992 by Viktor E. Frankl cit. page 100 Reprinted by permission of Beacon Press, ©2006 Beacon Press – Boston Massachusetts, 25 Beacon Street, Boston MA 02108-2892, www.beacon.org

[16] Sister Ruth Barrows OCD, *Essence of Prayer* (New York/Mahwah: Paulist Press, Inc. 2006). ISBN 978-15876-8039-7 (Used with publisher's permission.)

[17] Sandra M. Schneiders, *Prophets in Their Own Country* (Maryknoll: Orbis Books, 2011), cit. page 90 (Used with publisher's permission.)

[18] *New American Bible (Revised Edition)* (Washington, DC: Confraternity of Christian Doctrine, 2010, 1991, 1986, 1970), Matthew 3:31–32, Mark 4:30–32, Luke 13:18–19.

[19] Luke 8:4–15, Matthew 13:1–23, Mark 4:1–20.

[20] Luke 17:1–6.

[21] See Matthew 12:31–32 and Mark 3:28–29.

[22] Acts 10:1–44.

[23] Acts 10:44–46.

[24] Acts 11:1–18.

[25] Mark 2:27.

[26] John 21:15–17.

[27] John 14:15–17.

[28] Luke10:23–37 (See also Matthew 22:34–40 and Mark 12:28–34.)

[29] Billy Graham, *Hope for Each Day* (Nashville: Thomas Nelson, Inc., 2008), cit. September 16 © 2008 by Billy Graham (Used with publisher's permission.)

[30] John 3:16.

Chapter Two: Sacraments of Initiation

[31] Paulo Coelho, *Manuscript Found in Accra* (New York: Vintage Books, Random House LLC, 2012), cit. page 53.

Sacrament of Baptism

[32] Matthew 28:19–20, Luke 24:36–49, John 20:19–23, Acts 1:6–8.

[33] *New American Bible (Revised Edition)* (Washington, DC: Confraternity of Christian Doctrine, 2010, 1991, 1986, 1970).

[34] Richard Rohr, 'Immortal Diamond, The search for our true self,' ©2013 by Richard Rohr, cit. page x introduction, San Francisco, Jossey- Bass Publication, reprinted with permission of the publisher

[35] Rite of Baptism for Children, http://www.catholicliturgy.com/index.cfm/FuseAction/TextContents/Index/4/SubIndex/67/TextIndex/7

[36] Richard Rohr, 'Immortal Diamond, The search for our true self,' ©2013 by Richard Rohr, cit. page x introduction, San Francisco, Jossey- Bass Publication, reprinted with permission of the publisher

Sacrament of Confirmation

[37] Walter M. Abbott, SJ, General Editor, *Lumen Gentium* (New York: The America Press, 1966), cit. page 28, paragraph 11. (See also *Documents of Vatican II*.)

[38] Roman Ritual – Sacrament of Confirmation http://rclbsacraments.com/confirmation/walkthrough-confirmation-rite/ Copyright 2011 RCL Benziger Publishing, LLC. All Rights Reserved.

[39] "Prayer of Saint Teresa of Avila" (1515–1582), Catholicity, http://www.catholicity.com/prayer/prayer-of-saint-teresa-of-avila.html. access date 11/06/15.

[40] *New American Bible (Revised Edition)* (Washington, DC: Confraternity of Christian Doctrine, 2010, 1991, 1986, 1970), Mark 1:9–12. (See also Matthew 3:13–17; Luke 3:21, 22; Jn 129-34.)

[41] Ibid. Isaiah 11:2

[42] Ibid. Galatians 5:22, 25

[43] Ibid. Mark 1:9-12

Sacrament of Eucharist

[44] Excerpted from *Merton's Palace of Nowhere: A Search for God Through Awareness of the True Self* by James Finley. cit. page 45 Copyright ©1978, 2003 by Ave Maria Press®, Inc., P.O. Box 428, Notre Dame, IN 46556, www.avemariapress.com. Used with permission of the publisher.

[45] *New American Bible (Revised Edition)* (Washington, DC: Confraternity of Christian Doctrine, 2010, 1991, 1986, 1970), Luke 22:14–20.

[46] 1 Corinthians 11:23–26.

[47] Mark 14:10–21, Matthew 26:17–25, Luke 22:3–6, John 21–30.

[48] Mark 14:26–31, Matthew 26:30–35, Luke 22:31–34, John 13:36–38.

[49] Libreria Editrice Vaticana, *Catechism of the Catholic Church* (1994). (St. Justin, *Apol.* 1, 65–67:PG 6, 428–429.) http://www.newadvent.org/fathers/0126.htm

[50] Libreria Editrice Vaticana, *Catechism of the Catholic Church* (1994). (CCC 1328–1332.) http://www.usccb.org/beliefs-and-teachings/what-we-believe/catechism/catechism-of-the-catholic-church/epub/index.cfm

[51] Documents of Vatican II, *Lumen Gentium,* Walter M. Abbott, S.J. General Editor © 1966 The America Press, cit. page 28. All rights reserved. http://www.vatican.va/archive/hist_councils/ii_vatican_council/documents/vat-ii_const_19641121_lumen-gentium_en.html,paragraph 11

[52] *The New Roman Missal*, 3rd ed. (International Committee on English in the Liturgy, 2010). Washington, DC 20036-4101

[53] Richard Rohr, OFM, "Eucharist as Touchstone" 2000, Audio CD. Center for Action and Contemplation: 2007. cac.org PO Box 12464 Albuquerque, NM 87195, Used with permission of the publisher. Part Number ST-C-05

Chapter Three: Sacraments of Healing

[54] Myroslav Marynovych, "Reflections on Communist Crime and Punishment in the Light of the Ukrainian Revolution of Dignity," speech given at the Ruman-Reagan Award, Washington DC, June 11, 2014.

[55] Brief excerpts from pp.55-6, 57 from Pierre Teilhard de Chardin, *The Divine Milieu* © 1957 by Editions du Seuil. English translation Copyright © 1960 by William Collins Sons & Co., Ltd., London and Harper & Row, Inc., New York. Renewed © 1988 by Harper and Row Publishers, Inc. Reprinted by permission of HarperCollins Publishers.

[56] Atul Gawande, *Being Mortal, Medicine and What Matters in the End* (New York: Metropolitan Books, Henry Holt and Company).). © 2014 by Atul Gawande

Sacrament of Reconciliation

[57] William Barclay, *New Testament Commentary Revised Edition* cit. page 1 (First edition—Edinburgh: The Saint Andrew Press, 1956; Second edition 1958, revised edition 1975 by Westminster John Knox Press, Louisville,KY

[58] Hebrews 10:16–18.

[59] Jorge Mario Bergoglio (Pope Francis), *Reconciliation* Magnificat, vol. 14, no. 13, (March 2013): cit. page 76.

[60] Adapted from the *Marine Graduation Ceremony Booklet*, Marine Corps Recruit Depot, Parris Island, South Carolina, August 31, 2012.

Sacrament of Anointing of the Sick

[61] Atul Gawande, *Being Mortal, Medicine and What Matters in the End* (New York: Metropolitan Books, Henry Holt and Company). © 2014 by Atul Gawande

[62] Mark 2:1–12 and Matthew 9:1–8.

[63] Documents of Vatican II, *Lumen Gentium,* Walter M. Abbott, S.J. General Editor © 1966 The America Press, cit. page 28. All rights reserved, also cf. James 5:14-16

[64] Brief excerpts from pp.55-6,57 from Pierre Teilhard de Chardin, *The Divine Milieu* © 1957 by Editions du Seuil. English translation Copyright © 1960 by William Collins Sons & Co., Ltd., London and Harper & Row, Inc., New York. Renewed © 1988 by Harper and Row Publishers, Inc. Reprinted by permission of HarperCollins Publishers.

[65] David Baldacci, *'The Simple Truth'* [© 1998 by Columbus Rose Ltd. Warner Books, Inc. 1271 Avenue of the Americas, New York NY 10020, is reprinted with permission of the publisher – cit. pp. 510-511
.

[66] National Hospice and Palliative Care Organization 1731 King Street, Alexandria, Virginia 22314 (phone-703-837-1500) Website - *www.nhpco.org/ history-hospice-care/*

Chapter Four: Sacraments for Shepherding God's People

[67] Richard Rohr and John Bookser Feister, *Jesus' Plan for a New World,* St. Anthony Messenger Press, 1996 © Richard Rohr and John Bookser Feister, is reprinted with permission of the publisher – cit. page 19

[68] *The New Roman Missal,* 3rd ed. (International Committee on English in the Liturgy, 2010). Washington, DC 20036-4101

[69] New American Bible, revised edition © 2010, 1991, 1986, 1970 Confraternity of Christian Doctrine, Washington, D.C *Genesis 1:26-2870⁴* Ibid *Genesis 2:20b-24*

[70] Ibid Matt 28:16

[71] Catechism of the Catholic Church, Libreria Editrice Vaticana 1994. (CCC 1536)

Sacrament of Holy Marriage:

[72] Rev. William A. Anderson, *'In His Light'*– 2009 Houghton Mifflin Harcourt Religion Publishers, Orlando, Florida cit. page 177, reprinted with permission of the publisher.

[73]Ibid., cit. page 196.

209

74 *New American Bible (Revised Edition)* (Washington, DC: Confraternity of Christian Doctrine, 2010, 1991, 1986, 1970), 1 Corinthians 13:1–13.

75 John 2:1–10.

76 Paulo Coelho, *Manuscript Found in Accra* (New York: Vintage Books, Random House LLC, 2012), cit. page 6.

Sacrament of Holy Orders

77 Jorge Mario Bergoglio (Pope Francis), *In Him Alone Is Our Hope* (Yonkers: Magnificat Inc., 2013), cit. page 20.

78 Austen Ivereigh, *The Great Reformer* (New York: Henry Holt and Company LLC, 2014), cit. pp. 263–264.

79 Walter Brueggemann, *An Introduction to the Old Testament* (Louisville: Westminster John Knox Press, 2003), cit. pp. 4–5.

80 Luke 24:45–48.

81 "General Omar Bradley's Memorial Day Address," Omar N. Bradley, Guideposts, https://www.guideposts.org/positive-living/general-omar-bradleys-memorial-day-address.

82 *Address of Pope Francis to the participants in the plenary assembly of the international union of superiors general (i.u.s.g.)* Paul VI Audience Hall Wednesday, 8 May 2013 http://w2.vatican.va/content/francesco/en/speeches/2013/may/documents/papa-francesco_20130508_uisg.html

83 *New American Bible (Revised Edition)* (Washington, DC: Confraternity of Christian Doctrine, 2010, 1991, 1986, 1970), John 10:1–4.

84 HYMN OF THE UNIVERSE by Pierre Teilhard de Chardin. Copyright ©1961 by Editions du Seuil. English translation Copyright © 1965 by William Collins Sons & Co., Ltd., London and Harper & Row, Inc., New York. Reprinted by permission of Georges Borchardt, Inc., for Editions du Seuil.

Conclusion

[85] Anthony Esolen, *How The Church Has Changed The World*, Magnificat Vol. 16, No. 7, paraphrase cit. pp. 204-208, September 2014 Magnificat, Inc.86 Main Street, Yonkers NY 10701

[86] Rabbi Jonathan Sacks, *The Love That Brings New Life Into the World*, cit. page 14 Columbia Magazine, 1 Columbus Plaza. New Haven CT 06510, May 2015

[87] Dark Matter, dark energy, and cosmological constant - http://science.nasa.gov/astrophysics/focus-areas/what-is-dark-energy/ **NASA's John F. Kennedy Space Center and the Space Telescope Science Institute,** NASA Official: Kristen Erickson

[88] Ibid

[89] Ibid.

[90] Ibid.

[91] Father Alfred Delp, S.J. *Thy Kingdom Come* Magnificat,Vol. 16, No. 12,February 2015, cit. pp. 360-361 Magnificat, Inc.86 Main Street, Yonkers NY 10701

Appendix

[92] Thomas Merton, *Conjectures of a Guilty Bystander* (New York: Doubleday and Company, 1966), cit. page 7.

Our ability to believe is an awesome and empowering gift. It is the path to knowing and holds us in knowledge. It gives us courage to dream and to love. It allows us to go ever deeper into ourselves and into life. It takes us beyond the finite and opens for us glimpses of the infinite.

"Unless your Faith is Strong" attempts to identify our ability and need to believe as the source of empowerment to find meaning in every stage of our life…

…as young adults seeking meaning in the midst of family, friends, high school, changing familiar landscape (including separation), college, technical or military training and multiple career opportunities.

…as adults in mid-life seeking meaning again in family (but now as a parent, spouse, or adult child), friends (new and former), chosen career and transitioning careers.

…as adults in their later years continuing to seek meaning in family (perhaps now as grandparents), friends across generational lines transitioning into retirement, dealing with health issues and the death of family and friends.

"Unless your Faith is Strong…" attempts to identify the challenges and struggles common in life and the important role religious values and rites can play.

_____